FATHER

Will there still be priests in the Church's future?

Massimo Camisasca
Father. Will there still be priests in the Church's future?

Translated by Joseph T. Papa
Edited by Jonah Lynch

FRATERNITY
OF ST. CHARLES
Passion for the glory of Christ

Book design by Melissa Galliani
Layout by Fabrizio Cavaliere
cover photo: Elio e Stefano Ciol

Scripture quotations are translated by Joseph T. Papa from the Italian text cited by the author, in order to maintain shades of meaning which would otherwise be lost.

ISBN: 978-0-9823561-9-7

Massimo Camisasca

FATHER

Will there still be priests in the Church's future?

to Gianluca Attanasio
and Paolo Sottopietra

Contents

Foreword

During this Year of the Priest, I would like to collect the most important experiences and reflections of my past 25 years, during which I have been Superior of the Fraternity of St. Charles and, for much of that time, also rector of the seminary. I feel compelled to humbly offer to my brothers what God has given me to see and to understand.

The lives of many priests are marked by grave difficulties. At the same time, here and there we find vivid, positive signs to the contrary: priests who, mostly in obscurity, live their vocation with a sincere, quiet, daily dedication; saints whose names we don't know, who uphold the entire edifice of the Church. All of this fills us with gratitude to God and to these brothers. At the same time, we must not close our eyes to the difficulties that many others face.

Today, the problems are no longer ideological. Fortunately, the noisy diatribes over the priest's identity have almost disappeared. Still with us, however, are the abandonment, the loneliness of many priests, the loss of enthusiasm for a vocation meant to be fascinating and full of intense affectivity.

This book will not be a historical-sociological description of this crisis. Rather, I wish to outline the steps for a reform of priestly life. True, many problems come to us from the world outside of us, but the most serious obstacles are among and within us. Why, for example, are there so few formation directors who know how to lead young seminarians to self-awareness and confidence in God? Why are we convinced that the human sciences are enough? Why have we preferred to create liturgical enthusiasts, specialists in prayer, social action professionals – but not true men, mature men, men of God? Why does the study of philosophy and theology offer so many peripheral questions and *excurses*, hundreds of varied curiosities, but is unable to form intelligent adults, possessing a synthesis at once profound, essential, rigorous and free, nourished by the great Fathers and theologians and by the geniuses of humanity, from Plato to Von Balthasar? Why do we no longer know how to form people authentically fascinated by silence, reading, and study? These questions in one way or another pertain to us all, but impact directly the Church and her leaders.

Will there still be priests in the Church's future? Has not the time come for us to humbly inquire into the direction change should take?

I
Silence

An anchor is what keeps a boat from being tossed about by waves, wind and storms, from being driven to and fro. It provides a firm footing for the boat, though it may be miles from land. An invisible footing – but real, and experienced as such. For the priest, the anchor cannot be activity or action. Doing things or working can only be a genuine source of nourishment if, in the depths of our being, we know how to continually draw upon our relationship with God. Otherwise action will leave us empty, tired and, after intoxicating us, will end by destroying us.

I am convinced that this is a crucial point, indeed the decisive one, for a rebirth of priestly life. Activism is one of the most insidious threats to the life of a priest, because it can be easily confused with generosity, dedication to others, the gift of self or charity. How does it differ from these? Activism is superficial action: it sees problems, is aware of needs, looks to respond. The life of a priest who lives this way is often scattered in a variety of directions and works. His action is not in itself negative, but ends up so because it is short term, lasting only as long as his energy and sentiments. Hidden within activism, often unconsciously, is the illusion of saving others through what we do. Charity, on the other hand, moves us to enter God's action, collaborating in a work that precedes and surpasses us.

Being with God

The priest is a man called by God for the sake of others. He is not called by those others; rather, his response must be to God. To learn how to work for others, then, he must listen to God. This is the anchor: *he chose twelve, that they might be with him* (cf. Mk 3, 14). If we desire an authentic renewal of priestly life we must begin here, at the center, not the outskirts: with the personal relationship of every priest with Christ.

Overwhelmed by the problems, demands and expectations of those they serve, priests no longer have time to be with God – the One who called them. Obviously, one can be with God while being among people, which in fact is the mature, normal and definitive state. But to be with God among people, one must first learn to be with God, period. Even Jesus lived his first thirty years in the silence of Nazareth, learning there what would later characterize his public life. During the last three years of his life, he often withdrew from people to be alone. He spent entire nights in solitude (cf. Mt 21, 17). He took his disciples away from the crowds with him to rest. *Come with me for awhile, away from the clamor and demands of the crowd* (cf. Mk 6, 31) he said, teaching them to recollect themselves in his company.

There is something deeply human in all this, but also something tremendously revolutionary and countercultural. Our age fears silence, seeing it as a vacuum, as emptiness. People today immerse themselves in an overdose of stimulation. The television is on even at the dinner table. People are in contact with the whole world (or so they think) through the Internet. They go to dance clubs, with their numbing decibel levels, or seek more dangerous forms of escape. And all to avoid silence. Even when at home their focus is not inward, but projected beyond themselves.

But what does all this have to do with the life of the priest? What we have described is an atmosphere that infects everyone. Think of the cell phone, the computer, the new forms of presumed or real socialization, such as *Facebook*. I am not at all suggesting that we leave the world, or live like the Amish. The past isn't necessarily better than the present. Rather, I would desire that we participate in and benefit from our age. And it is precisely for this reason – so as to be able to benefit from this age of images and action – that we need to rediscover silence.

What is silence?

Throughout my life I have often asked myself what silence is. During the 1970's and 1980's I participated many times in the spiritual exercises of the *Memores Domini*,[1] preached by Fr. Giussani, who at the time was laying the foundations of that new community. I saw in him then a constant, almost obsessive insistence on the importance of silence, as if to say that without silence there is no Christian life, or even a truly human life.

But what is silence? Why is it so important for every person, and especially for every Christian, and finally, for every priest? How can a habit of silence mature in us?

---

[1] The ecclesial association Memores Domini was born out of the movement Communion and Liberation and was recognized by pontifical decree in 1988. Its members are lay people who desire to live their vocation to virginity within in the world of work.

Silence first of all brings to mind an absence of words and sounds. There is value in that, but we must not stop there. I do not desire silence so as to avoid hearing or seeing, to cut myself off from life. On the contrary, I want silence so as to be able to see more deeply and to hear the most important words, which are often suffocated or hidden, so as to linger over them. If silence demands a certain separation from the noise and racket of everyday life, it is in order to enter into reality more deeply and discover the true face of things, which is often hidden as behind a veil.

For the Christian, silence is the perspective through which faith looks at the things of the world. I am not saying that the Christian should be a visionary. Faith does not make him see imaginary or unreal things, but allows him to see more deeply the same things that everyone else sees. In contrast with Oriental philosophies and religions, in silence the Christian is not before a void, but before a personal "you".

The poet Clemente Rebora wrote this beautiful verse in his poem *The Poplar*: "And its trunk plunges into a truer place."[2] From my window I can see three small poplars. Every time I pass them I think of Rebora's words which, it seems to me, contain a suitable image of silence. We too, as people always have, often view life in fragments: this or that event, a word, something we hear on the news... Everything appears in isolation, and therefore without meaning. Silence, and faith, allow us to discover at least some connections between things, events and words. They allow us to perceive – even if still from afar, *as in a mirror, darkly* (1Cor 13, 12) – the face of him through whom every-

---

[2] C. Rebora, "Il pioppo", in *Le poesie*, Garzanti, Milan 1994, 297.

thing was made and to whom everything returns (cf. Act 17, 24-28; Col 1, 16). Only in silence are we able to grasp the meaning of the greatest things – sorrow and joy, love and work, beauty and suffering. And in silence, even the smallest things become meaningful.

Some years ago I saw one of the famous soprano Maria Callas's rare television interviews. Asked what was the most important thing she had learned about singing and wanted to pass on to others, she said something like: "Silence. All of the greatness in singing is in the silences between the words." I realized that this was not such a strange response when I heard it repeated by Giuseppe di Stefano, a great Italian tenor who died recently. When asked about the secret of his art in a radio interview, he said: "To pronounce all the words well, and do the silences properly".

Silence is not the absence of words, but the secret to discovering their true weight. I was impressed reading some words of Georges Simenon, the French novelist, creator of commissioner Maigret: the whole purpose of his writing was to disclose *the weight of things*. "To put a tree in the back of the garden |…| and to give to its leaves a certain weight, a certain presence |…| I believe I have found the word: presence. The presence of a piece of paper, of a bit of sky, of any object |…| If I may put it this way – the weight of life."[3]

When, before my ordination, I spent a week in complete silence at a Benedictine monastery on the outskirts of Milan, during my long hours in the cell I often looked at the ceiling. I had no books with me, or paper, only the wall to look at. I said to myself: "Perhaps, for a monk who passes

---

[3] G. Simenon, *L'età del romanzo*, Lucarini, Rome 1990, 32.

his whole life here, that mould, with its different patterns, could be a real companion." When we look persistently at things, they can speak. Even looking at a tree, one can glimpse the whole mystery of Being. If I were confined between four walls, for example, an airplane passing overhead would still be for me a symbol of my relation to the infinite.

Learning silence

I have discovered a striking definition: silence is our memory, filled with the awareness of belonging to Jesus.[4] If this is so, then it is clear that silence is anything but emptiness. Rather, it is the condition of dialogue with the One who is the center of the world and the secret face of all things.

Silence would be of no interest to me if it were not necessary for life. Through the years I have learned that it is more important than air or water; or at least, it is as necessary for our spirit as air and water are for our body. The Israelites had an expression: to see God's face – *your face, Lord, I seek* (Ps 27, 8). This saying is a beautiful image of what silence is: identification with the beloved. Silence is the present moment, indwelt by Another.

I would like to recount here a bit of how I discovered this. First of all, to learn silence one must be silent. Following the teachings of those who have been spiritual fathers to me, I dedicate an hour each day to a strict silence. I used to do this in the late afternoon. Gradually, I came to see that it was necessary to begin the day with

---

[4] Cf. *Direttorio della associazione ecclesiale "Memores Domini"*, pro manuscripto, 23.

silence, so I devote the first hour of my day to it. I was taught that we should begin the period of silence with a few minutes of prayer on our knees, perhaps before an image. It is a wonderful pedagogy to begin the day in adoration, gratefully recognizing the beauty of creation, God's goodness, the time given to us. The Father as the source of all. I don't want to be at all ingenuous, spiritualistic or abstract: there are nights when I don't sleep, other nights when I sleep only a little, mornings on which I awake beset by worries. It is precisely for this reason that to train my heart to see the beauty of life, to acknowledge the fatherhood that willed my existence, that willed the world into being and guides it, is the greatest good. Without silence it is impossible to discover God's fatherhood, to enter into God's movement that designs, day by day, to make us his own. We thus come to see that silence has a tremendous social value. Little by little, entering into the fatherhood of God and taking on Christ's perspective, my perspective on others begins to change. Like physical creation, but more so, others become a sign of Jesus. In this way the possibility of forgiveness, acceptance and living with others is born.

Then I pray, reading some *Hours* of the breviary. To begin prayer with the words Jesus taught us, or with the words with which he himself prayed, or those passed down to us by the Church, is an essential way of entering into that new perspective of which I just spoke. Meditating on the psalms, their words take on a certain weight, a truth of their own, speaking to me of things that have happened or are happening, helping me to recognize what is about me – truth and lies, friends and enemies –, giving a name to my hopes, teaching me to counsel and to console.

Meditative reading should always be a part of the hour of silence. Perhaps a page of Sacred Scripture or a text from the Fathers of the Church, the writings of a particular-ly meaningful and beloved saint, a text on spirituality, a book of Church history. Obviously, not all of these are of equal value, but they can all contribute to filling my silence with that light that will stay kindled the whole day long.

Regardless of what I have chosen to read as a help for my meditation, I must learn not to hurry. One cannot read Scripture or the works of a saint as he would a murder mys-tery – to see how it ends! Each word must be given its weight. Meditating on Scripture, I know that the word is inspired, that it was written to speak to me of Christ, to reveal his person to me, to draw me into his life, his thought. The entire Scripture, both the Old and the New Testaments, speaks to me of him. The time of meditation is not the time for exegesis or scholarly research, although a good exegetical text is always helpful. I must allow the words to penetrate, examining them to see what is behind them, the event they reveal. It is important on this count to know the different senses of Scripture: the historical, which we can never ignore; the allegorical, in which I see the face of Christ revealed in history through the types that prefig-ured him; the anagogical and the moral.

I linger over the words that most impress me: they are like a string that God has put in my hand to lead me to find the rest. Through meditation, I gradually discover the unity of all of Scripture, the Old Testament and the New. Indeed, I try to understand Scripture through Scripture itself. As Benedict XVI has written, the whole Bible has a direction, since there is an intimate connection between the Old and New Testa-ments. One must recognize the intimate unity of Scripture in order to understand the individual stretches of the road.[5] It

---

[5] Cf. J. Ratzinger - Benedict XVI, *Jesus of Nazareth*, Doubleday, New York 2007, 14.

is impossible to understand the New Testament deeply without knowing the Old: the history of salvation is one.

Scripture should be read as the Church reads it, in the context of the Church's life. It is a good thing, therefore, for the priest to begin with the texts proposed by the liturgy. This helps us to grasp the unity of Revelation, as well as the extraordinary relevance of the biblical texts for our daily life.

It is worthwhile to meditate on the commentaries that the Fathers of the Church have left us on the various books of Scripture: it is as though God wanted to give the Bible to us through them. They are called "Fathers", not just because they came before us, but because, through their lives and works, they left us a privileged experience of Christian wisdom. They read the deposit of faith as men of their own era, responding to the questions of their contemporaries. As a result, they have provided us with a varied, but unified synthesis that merits the attention of all.

Then, the saints. Especially their writings, although without ignoring their lives, when we find a version that is not overly apologetic or saccharine. We need to be able to see in the saints a path that we too can follow.

Finally, the study of Church history. We are a people that lives in history. Without a knowledge of the events our people have lived through we cannot truly understand ourselves. We should therefore choose a history of the Church written by an author who loves the Church. In the Church's history – in the events it has lived through, including sins and errors, steps forward and advances in holiness – we will see the reflection of our personal history and find light for our priestly ministry.

There is also a place in my silence for recitation of the rosary. As when I pray the psalms, this simple gesture turns my silence into a wonderful preparation for the whole day.

Almost without noticing it, I think of the people I will meet. I ask God, and Mary, to inspire me with responses to their questions, for the right tone of voice. I ask them to enable me to listen and to welcome, to make me strong and wise, so I can take those I meet by the hand and accompany them where God wants them to go. I also ask for the grace to bear setbacks, the frustration I experience when I can't find the right words, when problems seem to have no solution, when the heart of another seems hopelessly closed.

In conclusion: in silence one learns, little by little, to enter into the will of God, thus fulfilling the invocation of the Our Father: *thy will be done* (Mt 6, 10). How do we discover God's will for ourselves and others? And how do we keep to it? Through the years, through many falls, through much forgetfulness and weariness, gradually silence causes a new perspective to be born in us – more like Christ's, less worldly, making us able to help those entrusted to us. Our whole day changes. To live silence is thus the beginning of fulfillment: a quiet experience of peace that makes silence desirable.

In addition to the daily hour of silence, my life is sprinkled with days or longer periods in which most of the day is spent in silence. I am thinking of the days of retreat at the beginning of the various liturgical seasons (Advent, Lent, Pentecost), or of the spiritual exercises which, whether I preach them or only participate, are always a tremendous source of nourishment for my life.

Silence and action

When silence is real, it can transform the way we live our day. If I don't let the world into my silence, I can make my silence enter the world. That is, I can look at my own life, and that of others, with more hope and more truth, more sympathy and more depth.

It is not true that silence removes us from action. On the contrary, it generates in us a new capacity to accept, to love, to offer ourselves for others. I once said to my priests that silence is an action of God in our lives: it is our action, indwelt by Another. An Other indwells our time, giving it form. Silence is not an absence of affection: rather, it is the presence of Love. It gradually causes a passage from a false reality that I have imagined, to the true, definitive reality, in which the colors, tastes and loves are authentic and known for what they truly are.

I try to not to give up my morning hour of silence too easily. Faithfulness to prayer creates a *habitus* through which every moment of time, every encounter of the day, tends to become, literally, prayer.

The new technologies

The effect of silence on our day can also be measured by the many decisions that we make regarding the use of our time. For example: how much time goes to watching television? Some might laugh: television programs are so banal – when they aren't dreadful, like reality shows – that it's not even worth talking about. Believe me, it is. Many priests come home at night alone, tired. Television becomes a form of companionship, by default more than by choice. Its images stay in our minds and hearts, sending us to bed disturbed and tired. At every stage of life, we must learn to be careful with television and to choose. In the houses of my community, I ask a particular attention regarding this of all my priests. I would rather have them watch a film together. Also, the television set should be in a common area, not in the bedroom or study.

All of this is compounded today by the existence of new technological tools. I am fully aware of the importance of the Internet and other similar communications media – in many cases they are truly necessary for one's work. For a priest, however, are they always so vital? Do we make good judgments concerning the amount of time we spend in front of the computer? Even if we are unaware of it, technology introduces a different perspective on things and people. It can cause us to lose our wonder and lead to an activist mentality, where what counts is to get a lot done, quickly. By the same token, the power of pornography is a mystery to no one, not only what is explicitly intended as pornography, but also that which, practically unnoticed, dominates the common mentality and exerts a constant pressure on people's lives, precisely through technology. I read a recent American statistic that sixty to seventy percent of Internet use is for pornography. Priests are not angels: they are men, and their freedom is fragile. We should do everything, then, to help priests toward an intelligent and attentive use of technology.

The education of freedom

These new and invasive forms of communication underscore the fundamental importance of an education of freedom, which should take place during the years of seminary, though not stopping there. Every priest – like every person – is brought back to the basic question: what do I desire for myself? From where do I expect the good for my life and for my happiness? What paths can foster and assure this? At a certain point in his life Fr. Giussani had a brilliant intuition. He said that every true possession requires a distance – that is, a sacrifice.[6] Just as to look at a painting one can't stand with his nose against the canvas, so to live in reality a certain distance, or vigilance, is necessary. We should continually ask ourselves: what am I looking for? Whom do I want to encounter, to see? Who can make me happy?

---

[6] "The highest form of human life is possession that includes detachment", cf. L. Giussani, «Tu» (o dell'amicizia), BUR, Milan 1997, 135.

II
Prayer

Silence opens the way to prayer. I could have dealt with both of these experiences in a single chapter, but I wanted to distinguish them because, in fact, prayer without preparation can become the repetition of memorized phrases, a ritual, a duty from which our hearts, our questions and the most pressing hopes of our lives are excluded. It is not without reason that the Bible counsels: *Before praying, prepare your soul, so you would not be like one who tempts God* (cf. Sir 18, 23). Silence is thus the essential vestibule of prayer. How many times do we – especially we priests – begin Holy Mass, or morning or evening prayer, without the slightest pause, not even a moment of quiet! By so doing, we carry into our prayer the weight of everything we have been living only a few seconds before.

What is prayer?

Jesus says: *Let anyone who thirsts come to me and drink* (Jn 7, 37). This phrase, *anyone who thirsts*, speaks to us of our life moved by desire. In the *Letter to Proba* St. Augustine says that, in our prayer, God wants our desire to be exercised.[7] Without desire, we won't ask. Someone who is not thirsty does not

---

[7] Cf. Augustine, *Letter* 130 *to Proba*, 14.25 - 15.28.

desire a drink, nor does he go near the spring, nor is he even attracted by it. God's attractiveness needs to find a correspondence in us. If our prayer is preceded by real silence, over time our deepest questions will more easily break through our distractions and problems.

Like silence, we need prayer to live. Often as I have grown older I have found myself asking what is truly necessary for life. I have wanted to focus my heart, not on details, but on what is essential. In doing so, I have discovered that what is necessary is also free: what we need most is at the same time a gift, as with biological life, the life of the soul, freedom, love.

Reflecting on myself, I discover this truth in the deepest part of my consciousness: "I did not make myself. I have received life, and receive it continually, every day." When I experience this transparency of myself to myself, I begin to pray. Prayer, in fact, is nothing other than the petition that springs forth from my consciousness of being a creature, of my continual need to be drawn from nothingness into existence. Prayer means above all to ask, to ask God for what we need.

Here I find the deepest and most comprehensive characteristic of my priestly life. I have been called by God to be a priest, through the Church, before and above all else to pray.

Prayer is not a tax that a priest has to pay so as to able to do other things. It can at times seem this way in the lives of some priests: one must pray, absolving this duty as quickly as possible, so as to go out among the people to do what really counts. The mistake is in considering oneself the source of salvation, while at the same time having a reductive, spiritualistic view of prayer.

The priest, rather, is above all a man of prayer. This means that he is called to be the voice of his fellow human beings before God. My prayer is never individual. Every petition I make to God gathers within it the cries, the hopes, the supplication, the thanksgiving of all the people in the world: of those who believe and those who don't believe, those who know of my prayer and those who don't. God desires that not even the smallest sigh be lost.

I cannot, however, live this essential task of my priesthood, this cosmic reality of prayer, if I don't first learn how to pray. To learn to pray means to learn what we should ask for and how we should ask. And even before that, it means to learn to whom it is that we address our requests.

St. Thomas takes up two definitions of prayer: to ask for right things, and to raise the soul to God.[8] Both of these definitions come from a consideration of the *Our Father*, the only prayer taught to us by Jesus. It is the form of every other prayer, and contains the definitive revelation of God to humanity.

Father, says St. Luke, with infinite simplicity (cf. Lk 11:2). If we do not have this awareness, at least in the depths of our consciousness, of speaking to the Father, to God who is Father, we cannot pray. Prayer is not thoughts about God, but a participation in God's history with humanity. Prayer is therefore a dialogue, not the repetition of a *mantra* before the void. Even if the words have been commanded, they always arise anew on the lips of one who prays in a personal and attentive way. If we enter, even from a distance, into the fatherhood of God, the generous author of all things and of every human being and the one who saves us, forgiving our sins, we will discover the meaning of the

---

[8] Cf. Thomas Aquinas, *In Psalmos*, Proemium; pars 24, n. 11; *Summa Theologiae*, II-II, q. 83, aa. 1, 5 e 17.

seven petitions of the *Our Father*. Three ask God that He be acknowledged and loved, and the whole world molded by his presence. Four invite us to ask the Father for our needs: material and spiritual bread, pardon for our sins, deliverance from temptation and from evil.

In the light of these petitions, every other request becomes possible. *We, in fact, do not know what we should ask for* (cf. Rm 8, 26), and yet we are invited by Jesus to ask always, to ask with persistence and faithfulness – but also to accept that our request might be fulfilled differently than how we would wish. Through prayer we put ourselves in tune with God, we find ourselves on his wavelength.

Only if a priest experiences this training will he, little by little, become the intermediary of the voices and hopes of humanity towards God.

Prayer and work

There is nothing worse for a priest than to experience an opposition between prayer and activity, between prayer and work – as if prayer itself were not a fundamental and demanding work for the priest. Not without reason did St. Benedict call prayer the *opus Dei*: God's work in us, and our work toward God.[9]

I know well how difficult and full of challenges a priest's life can be, and how arid some days are. But if we wait until we feel like it to pray, we will gradually stop praying. And the extinguishing of prayer is the beginning of the extinguishing of priestly life. Pray even when you don't feel like

---

[9] Cf. Benedict of Nursia, *Rule*, XLIII.

it, even when everything seems dry, distant, when the words seem lifeless: if we remain faithful to our external practices of prayer, it will eventually blossom in our interior. As with every love, it is faithfulness that reawakens feeling.

Prayer of Intercession

Prayer leads us to the discovery of the mysterious and profound unity with which God has united all human beings, the deepest essence of which is intercession. To intercede, to ask on behalf of another, is the prerogative of a person who is in tune with God's mercy.[10] By the grace of baptism, his heart becomes the place where supplication moves between earth and heaven.

When I pray, I am convinced of being a successor of Moses, who raised his hands during the battle and offered his sacrifice for all the people (cf. Ex 17, 8-14). In this way we understand that prayer is really an action. Most of all, it bears within it the voices of others. It involves listening to and reaching out to others, being interested in them, feeling them as part of oneself. Then, it becomes a taking of others by the hand to bring them to God, an offering of oneself for others.

All of this takes place in a sublime way during the Mass. But all prayer is intercession. When I pray, I petition God for those who are unable to speak to him, for those who don't know how to pray, those who have stopped praying or have never learned how. Every priest brings the mystery and the lives of all people before Christ.

---

[10] Cf. *Catechism of the Catholic Church*, n. 2635

In my prayer, I see again and again the faces of those closest to me – my parents, friends, acquaintances, those who have asked me to pray for them. As when, saying the *Angel of God* before bed, I make a spiritual journey through all the houses of my community throughout the world. Prayer is silence, populated with names.

The Liturgy of the Hours

One of the most precious treasures passed down by the Church to priests, and indeed to all the faithful, is the *Book of Psalms*. In the course of a week, the 150 psalms provide the framework for monastic prayer. For priests, and for lay people who take part in this prayer, they are spread over a month. Until Vatican II the liturgy of the hours was said in Latin, and was much more burdensome than it is now. In addition to Lauds and Vespers, it called for Prime (now eliminated) and the obligatory recitation of Terce, Sext and None (whereas now one can choose just one of these three). Moreover, the psalms were quite difficult in Latin, with the result that the liturgy of the hours could frequently become mechanical, a duty, a task to be fulfilled because to omit it was a mortal sin. This is no longer the case. The liturgy of the hours is said in the vernacular, which is a tremendous help in remembering it throughout the day – in keeping vigil in heart and mind, identifying ourselves with the hours of the day as Jesus lived them, with the rhythm of his earthly and heavenly existence.

The liturgy of the hours includes readings from the Old and New Testaments, prayers and hymns, but especially, as I have said, the reading of the psalms. They are an absolutely unique form of prayer. Mostly attributed to

David the king, they are in fact the work of a number of authors who have gathered in their poetry the infinite facets of the human soul before God. In them we find the believer, the doubter, the rebel; one who makes supplication, one in trials or despair, and one who rejoices over being set free.

In this way, the voices of the various moments of the praying person's life can reach God. At the same time, people of every time and place find a voice. If the psalm asks me to sing a song of praise when I am sad, I become the voice of those who rejoice. At other times when I don't have special needs or pressing problems, the dramatic words of a psalm become the expression of so many men and women, weeping and crying out in the various countries of the world. Every day, and at every moment, the unity of the human race before God takes a step forward through the liturgy of the hours.

The praying of the psalms, moreover, is not just the prayer of an individual, or the prayer of the human community through him. It is also and above all the prayer of Jesus. As the Gospels testify, the psalms were the Old Testament text most often cited by Jesus. He prayed the psalms in the synagogue, and before his death he spoke to the Father with a psalm. For this reason we are certain of the efficacy of our prayer. In the liturgy of the hours we not only pray to Jesus, but Jesus himself prays to the Father for us.

If the psalms reveal God to man, and man to himself, we can also say that they reveal God to himself. They assume the rhythm of a dialogue in which man inquires of God, and vice versa. Each expresses himself by recounting, by questioning, and at times even by accusing the other. Sometimes God gives in to our pleas: he makes our requests his own, incorporating them into his plan and

showing us that there is room in God even for us; he mit-
igates his punishments, revealing himself as mercy.

The communal nature of the liturgy of the hours is best
expressed when it is prayed with others, when a priest is
joined by his brothers priests or by lay people. This should
be done if possible once or twice a day, or at least some
days during the week.

This discovery of the psalms did not happen right away
in my priestly life. It was years before I became aware of
their importance and usefulness. They have become a
tremendous help for me in saying Mass without distraction
– both as a preparation, and as a continuation after Mass of
the Eucharistic sacrifice. I found this same awareness in
some words of John Paul II. In dialogue with André
Frossard, he said: "Everyone knows that the priest's day is
liturgical, not only thanks to the Mass but also through the
liturgy of the hours, which confers on the day its special
rhythm. On the whole, work takes most of the time, but all
activities should be rooted in prayer as though in a spiritual soil. The depth of this soil must not be too thin."[11]
Nowadays, if I have to put off some part of my prayer, I feel
out of place, a bit dazed, like when I get up in the morning
without having had enough sleep.

Eucharistic adoration

In recent years I have discovered the importance of
Eucharistic adoration. The time I spend before the
Eucharist in my chapel has never been without fruit. It has

---

[11] A. Frossard - John Paul II, «Be not afraid!», The Bodley Head, London 1984, 3.

allowed me to understand many things about myself and about the world, about Christ, and finally about the Father.

First of all, Eucharistic adoration always brings me into the silence of God the creator, when everything voicelessly came forth from his hands – something like what happened at Bethlehem, and before then at Nazareth, at the moment of Mary's *yes*. Through adoration, a revolution takes place in my mind and in my life. I understand that what matters most – God himself – lives in silence.

Before the Eucharist, I learn that He agreed to accept the risk of being ignored and trampled upon. This teaches me much about the method of my ministry. It shows me that the things of God are born in secret and develop according to a logic different than the world's. Silence and hiddenness: I can enter in this way into the reality of the baptism of babies, and that of confession – that secret moment when forgiveness occurs –, into the reality of suffering and death, but also that of the resurrection, which took place in the stillness of dawn, seen only by the angels.

Through adoration, I also enter into the carnality of Christianity. The invisible God agreed to assume the species of bread; he agreed to become food, so as to transform our lives from within. In this way, through adoration, I understand a bit more who God is: his condescension, his identification with our humanity, his giving himself into our hands. He shared our life, that it might flourish from within. In the same way, we priests are sent to share the life of our fellow human beings, to ask with them that it be enlightened and transformed.

I have said and written often that, for me, Eucharistic adoration is like a university course. It is a dialogue in which I always learn something new: my being a creature as compared with the immensity of God, his providence and wisdom, my need for humility and trust. And in adoration, the recollection of the faces of those I love, to bring them to God, becomes even more vivid.

The rosary

One of my earliest memories is of our big kitchen, with the fireplace lit. In the evening we gathered around the fire to say the rosary, always in Latin. I was not obliged to participate – I was only four or five years old – but I often followed along in at least some of the prayers. As a grown-up and a priest, I rediscovered the rosary through the Marian fervor of John Paul II. Fr. Giussani also had us say a decade of the rosary during summer vacations in the mountains when I was in high school, while we were taking in the awesome spectacle of the Alps – it was a form of contemplation. John Paul II emphasized the contemplative value of the rosary, which we say explicitly: "In the first mystery we contemplate…".[12] John Paul, who said "the Rosary is my favourite prayer,"[13] repeated these words of Paul VI in his apostolic letter on the holy rosary: "Without contemplation, the Rosary is a body without a soul, and its recitation runs the risk of becoming a mechanical repetition of formulas [...] By its nature the recitation of the Rosary calls for a quiet

---

[12] TRANSLATOR'S NOTE: In saying the rosary, Italians introduce each mystery with the following expression (e.g.): "In the first joyful mystery we contemplate the annunciation of the angel Gabriel to the Blessed Virgin Mary." In English we might use "meditate on" in this context. J.T.P.

[13] John Paul II, *Angelus*, October 29, 1978.

rhythm and a lingering pace."[14] For me, like the liturgy of the hours, the rosary is a preparation for and contunuation of the Mass. Through it I learn to live the various moments of Jesus' life, very often through Mary's eyes. Mary is a mother for every Christian, but especially for priests: she points out the way, brings us to Jesus and helps us to follow him.

John Paul II invited us to treasure precisely this contemplative dimension of the Marian prayer. The words of the Hail Mary follow one another almost without our being aware of it. The intentions of our prayer are expressed and then abandoned to the mercy of God, while we focus our attention on the person of Jesus.

The rosary is a simple prayer. It can be said anywhere, at any moment of the day, in whatever condition our soul happens to be. If someone is short on time or gets easily distracted, he can spread the five decades out over the day. For me the rosary is like a chain that binds me to God and to many, many people, a point of unity between the present, the past and the future of the Church and of the world. "The ancient principle of *contemplata aliis tradere*[15] is always contemporary and life-giving", wrote John Paul II. For him, the priest "he is entitled to communicate – uniquely and exclusively – only *contemplata*, thoughts passed through prayer."[16]

---

[14] John Paul II, *Rosarium Virginis Mariae*, n. 12.
[15] "What you have contemplated, comunicate to others."
[16] A. Frossard ... , *op. cit.*, 34.

III
The Liturgy

The liturgy is the highest form of prayer. It contains all other prayers in itself, and all other prayers take their meaning from it.

During the liturgical celebration, priest and faithful speak with their own voices, but they say words commanded by Jesus, through the Church's tradition. The words are not theirs alone: they are above all Christ's.[17] Likewise, the gestures and actions are at once those of men and those of Jesus. This is why the liturgy – when it is faithful to the intention with which it was instituted – is a prayer whose efficacy is certain.

In the liturgy Christ makes himself known to us, he gives himself to us. He becomes the center of our existence, our mind and our action, thus shaping our lives. The liturgy is the school *par excellence* for both our being and our knowledge. Participating in it, we take part in the new life that Jesus brought to earth.

Liturgical action involves words, songs, colors, gestures and bodily positions. In this way faith is revealed not only as a collection of truths to be believed, but as a new life that is given to us and which elevates our intelligence and our senses. The liturgy also combats our temptation to activism only if we recollect ourselves, entering into the

---

[17] Cf. *Sacrosanctum Concilium*, n. 7.

action that Jesus does with us and for us, can we be with and for others effectively. Otherwise, we will only bring to others the emptiness that we ourselves live.

What is the liturgy?

In a certain way, the liturgy is the continuation of the Incarnation, the living out of the life and mysteries of Jesus in the world of today. In it, the priest experiences the relationship with the risen Lord as something extremely concrete, capable of sustaining his entire life. The Lord's desire to be present in history was manifested by his earthly life, and then after his resurrection through the gift of the Spirit: uniting people to himself, making them partakers of his very life through the gifts of baptism, the other sacraments and the various charisms that form his people. Christ is the protagonist of the liturgy. Only by accepting him as the protagonist, can we in turn become protagonists. This thought, over time, has engendered in me a fitting sobriety in liturgical celebration, an essentiality that lets the One who indwells the liturgy shine forth. Even the tone of voice and the calmness and measure with which the gestures are done is important. But most important of all is to never depart from what the Church has passed down through the centuries.

Participating in the liturgy in this manner teaches us to love beauty. In the liturgy, that definitive world to which we are all destined appears as in filigree. In celebrating it, we must never forget its cosmic infinitude, which reaches to the farthest ends of creation and includes the angels in heaven and the saints of every age. The liturgy is eternity entering time and space, the world as God conceived of it.

It gives new meaning to the year and to the week, to forms of liturgical space and works of art.

Is there any need to speak of the importance of beauty? It is enough to think of the cathedrals, the paintings, the sacred sculptures that mark two thousand years of Christian history and the precious objects (chalices, patens, etc…) it has produced. Sacred art today, especially architecture, is seeking a new equilibrium after the disorientation that followed Vatican II. The evil that has resulted from entrusting the construction of so many important churches to non-believing architects is obvious to everyone. The one criteria for the architectural design of a new church should be: does this help the celebration of the liturgy and prayer? All else takes its meaning from this.

Through active participation in the liturgy, our heart is remade: forgiven, we become partakers of the dimensions of the very heart of Christ, and we too are now able to forgive. We learn in the liturgy that love is the primary, the only true reality, and that it will also be the last and definitive reality.[18] Even our work enters the liturgy, receiving from it its meaning and proper direction. Recall the offertory prayer: "We have this bread to offer, which earth has given and human hands have made (…) this wine to offer, fruit of the vine and work of human hands."[19] All our labor – of those present, of those we know, of our acquaintances – is brought to the altar and becomes the material for man's offering to God. God's objectivity penetrates every

---

[18] Cf. M. Camisasca, *Terra e Cielo*, Cantagalli, Siena 2006, 26. The book is dedicated to the themes developed in this chapter.

[19] Cf. *Preghiera della presentazione dei doni*, in *Messale Romano*, Libreria Editrice Vaticana, Vatican City 1983, 308 - 309.

detail of our human subjectivity, transforming it and draw-
ing it to himself.

To conclude, the liturgy becomes the heart of Christian
education. First, because it affirms the primacy of God in
human life. Second, because it reveals his presence
through the ordinary things of life. And finally, because it
involves those present in listening, doing and seeing, participation in a dynamic event that involves all the dimensions of the personality. We find the clearest expression of
what the liturgy is in a preface of the Christmas Mass: as
we encounter God visibly, give us a taste for that which
does not pass away.[20] Through our participation in the
sacraments and the prayers we live already in the new
world, though still immersed in time.

Singing

Singing is an integral, and therefore indispensable, part of
liturgical celebration. Through its remarkable unity of
word, rhythm and melody, it is the privileged path for
entering into the mystery the Church celebrates. In this
sense, a song is true precisely when it leads one into the
mystery. The choice of songs, therefore, must consider this
objective dimension: not everything is appropriate, or at
least not for every occasion. Singing gives color, weight
and attractiveness to the words, and manifests our understanding of our relationship with Christ. One only sings
from his living, personal experience of God.

---

[20] Cf. *Prefazio di Natale* I, in Ivi, 316.

I am convinced that an adequate education in singing is a primary responsibility for a priest who wants to foster a spirit of prayer and adoration in his people.

Until the Sixties, at least in Italy, singing was reduced to popular songs in devotional processions, or rare moments during the Eucharistic celebration. Almost no one knew Gregorian chant, except the *Salve Regina* and the Eucharistic hymns. Even when new songs for Mass began to be written in the second half of the twentieth century, few had the courage to return to the psalms or the words of Scripture. The most important exception to this was Father Gelineau, the foremost advocate of psalmody after the Council.[21] And of course there were other songs, mostly written in the context of the movements, that did express the words of the psalms or hymns to the Virgin in a musical form combining creativity and tradition.

My experience during these 25 years in the seminary of the *Fraternity of St. Charles* has convinced me that Gregorian chant is the ideal form of every liturgical song. "It should therefore tend to inform all other songs."[22] Like no other vocal expression, from its beginnings Gregorian chant has expressed the calm, glad certainty of faith, the joy of salvation, the communion of brothers in one voice before God. Everything that moves to prayer – and thus all other types of liturgical song – must be referred to its balance and essentiality. Nothing expresses the celebratory aspect of the liturgy, its rich atmosphere of hope and restrained joy,

---

[21] The Jesuit priest Joseph Gelineau (1921-2008) dedicated his life to liturgical chant.

[22] Cf. Benedict XVI, *Meeting with Representatives from the World of Culture*, Collège des Bernardins, Paris, September 12, 2008.

43

like Gregorian chant, and nothing expresses the liturgy as the supreme repose in life as it does.

Liturgical song is not born of an individual creativity that seeks to express the self. Rather, it is a prayer that blossoms into melody. One must "vigilantly recognizing with the 'ears of the heart' the inner laws of the music of creation [...] and thus discovering music that is worthy of God, and at the same time truly worthy of man, music whose worthiness resounds in purity."[23]

The Vatican II reform

As a borderland between time and eternity, the liturgy is subject to two temptations: on the one hand that of fixity, and on the other that of excessive change. After centuries of celebration in Latin and long-established norms, and after the discreet but courageous reforms carried out by Pius X through Pius XII, the post-conciliar period saw an avalanche of changes. Some of these were truly necessary: reform of the liturgy of the hours, proclamation of the biblical texts in the vernacular, a more abundant access to Scripture, the simplification of some celebrations... Others, however, represented a grave abandonment of the prior tradition. In preaching, as in the celebration of the Mass itself, the sacrificial value of the Mass was obscured, in favor of an emphasis on its being a communion meal. The total abandonment of Latin, which could have been preserved at least in the canon of the Mass (as specified by the Council), contributed to a reduction of the sacred-

---

[23] *Ibidem*.

ness of the liturgical act in the eyes of the faithful. The translation of the prayers and Scriptural texts, not always well done and at times a downright betrayal of the original, brought an impoverishment of the faith, not to mention the subjection of the people of God to the arbitrariness of exegetes and theologians. Before our very eyes, we have witnessed the trivialization of the liturgical celebration in many communities.

The sacred is God's holiness, reaching us through the celebration of the holy mysteries. The Christian mystery, moreover, is not what is incomprehensible, but what is infinite and infinitely knowable: it is the Infinite in time. We are a long way from the luminous age of the Fathers of the Church, who made the mystery the center of their preaching, their pedagogy and their gratitude to God. All of this, in fact, has stirred up a traditionalist minority which for some time has identified obedience to the tradition with simple fixedness of norms. If the liturgy becomes an escape into God that removes us from people or, conversely, a bowing to people that removes us from God, everything loses its truth. This is particularly true for the priest celebrant, but ends up involving everyone entrusted to him. Only by truly entering into God, by entering into his action, can we truly be with others. To enter into God – who is gift – allows us to draw near, with him, to a humanity in need of healing.

What, then, is to be done? The teaching of Benedict XVI contains the guidelines for responding to this question. For the Holy Father, the main characteristic of the liturgical event is beauty. To enter into beauty means to enter into God who is communion, self-gift. This beauty shines in creation, in the election of the chosen people, and finally in the revelation of Jesus. This is the liturgy for Benedict XVI:

"The truest beauty is the love of God, who definitively revealed himself to us in the paschal mystery."[24]

We are not dealing, therefore, with a desacralization of our celebration, but with understanding what *sacred* really means. In celebrating Mass and the sacraments, an awareness of God's greatness should grow in us, and of the impossibility of his being reduced to our schemes, concepts or expectations. The sacred is not the arcane, shrouded in a mysterious logic reserved to a few. It is mysterious precisely because it is infinitely near us. God's incomprehensibility is a result, not of his distance from us, but of the infinite depth of his love. To foster a sense of the sacred means education in solemnity, in calmness and in the delightful awareness that what is occurring allows us to enter, with patience, into the logic of the other: to listen to and respect Him for who he is, not imposing our own words which would be mere chatter, arbitrariness, idiosyncrasy. In silence we learn where the daring of love, and innovation, can take us.

What place do the rubrics and norms have in the liturgy? They are important because they convey to us an ancient tradition, often going back to the Church's first centuries. When I reread the prayers of the missal, especially in Latin, I enter an experience of Christianity that leads me to the Fathers, the saints, the great moments in Church history, all of which makes obedience to the rubrics not only understandable, but even desirable. Unfortunately today one hears additions or arbitrary changes during celebration of the Mass and the sacraments. I must say that, in my long experience, I have never heard a change that improves on

---

[24] Benedict XVI, *Sacramentum Caritatis*, n. 35.

the original. This stands to reason, since it is almost impossible that an individual, improvising during the celebration, could draw on a wisdom deeper than the sedimentation of two thousand years of history.

The risks of the post-Council period

The entrusting of the liturgy to "experts" has involved great risks for the whole Church. We cannot live on liturgy alone, precisely because we receive our life from the liturgy. The tendency to take refuge in rites often derives, especially in young priests, from a fear of life and history. Thus the liturgical celebration, even saying the breviary, become ends in themselves. Priests become specialists in vestments, rituals and censings, thus entirely losing the sense of what the liturgy is really meant to be for the Christian people. Liturgical celebration is never an end in itself but, as the Council rightly said, it is *culmen et fons*,[25] that is, the place that both teaches communion and is the privileged expression of it. A liturgy that is closed in on itself, that celebrates itself, enamored of its own beauty, is not a Christian liturgy.

The decades after the Council also witnessed a political reduction of the liturgy. Holy Mass became not only the place where the differences between celebrant and people were blurred, but also the place for social declarations. One example could be the *democratization* of the liturgy, which derives from an egalitarian corruption of the idea of communion. The priest came to be thought of as someone

---

[25] Cf. *Sacrosanctum Concilium*, n. 10.

elected by the assembly, and thus easily replaceable. It is certainly true that the priest represents the assembly before God, but we must not forget that in the first place he represents God before the assembly.

This sort of reduction is inacceptable in the liturgy. Its true political significance is the establishment of the kingdom of God, as the advent of justice. The liturgy is a source of justice because it opens the way to reconciliation with the God revealed and given to us as Father, which teaches us charity towards our brothers and sisters.

IV
The Mass

"Without the priest Our Lord's passion and death would be useless."[26] These words of the Cure of Ars, which could seem "exaggerated", as Benedict XVI himself noted,[27] are in fact enlightening, and not only for an understanding of the greatness of the priest. They are also a help to priests in discovering the center of their life and mission. "Oh, how great is the priest |...|; if he understood this, he would die |...| God obeys him: he says two words, and Our Lord descends from heaven at the sound of his voice, enclosing himself in a tiny host."[28]

John Paul II was also deeply convinced of the absolute relationship that exists between the priesthood and the Eucharist: "The priesthood exists because Christ *left in the Church, in the Eucharist,* his sacrifice, the sacrifice of his body and blood."[29]

All the other dimensions of the priest's mission (preaching, fatherhood, self-gift for the people...) begin here. The priest is a man chosen by God above all for the

---

[26] B. Nodet, Le curé d'Ars. Sa pensée – Son coeur, Foi Vivante, 1966, 100.

[27] Cf. Benedict XVI, Letter of His Holiness Pope Benedict XVI Proclaming a Year for Priests on the 150th Anniversary of the "Dies Natalis" of the Curé of Ars, Vatican City 2009, 6.

[28] B. Nodet, op. cit., 97.

[29] A. Frossard..., op. cit., 148.

eucharistic sacrifice. He is the intermediary, in time and space, of the memorial of Jesus' sacrifice.

The heart of the day

The Mass is the heart of my day. Thirty years ago, right after my ordination, I didn't have this awareness, which is something that takes more than study to acquire. Certainly theology can enlighten, but much more useful are the words and experiences of the saints. What does it mean that the Mass is the center of the day? Even today I am not always ready to take on the weight of that celebration, nor do tiredness, worries and distractions magically disappear. I am conscious, however, that the celebration of Mass is the most important thing that I have to do during the day, and that all the other hours of the day are connected to it, as by invisible threads.

Above all, the Mass is the work of God. The most valuable thing that I have to do every day is thus to adhere to the work done by Another. I don't save the world with my words or my actions. This recognition has caused a genuine revolution in my understanding of myself, of others, of the world and of time.

At the Mass I celebrate each day, not only do those present "participate," but, through me, so do all of the people that I will see that day, all those who will ask something of me for themselves or their loved ones, all those whose dramas I will learn of from the radio or the newspaper. Those close to me also participate: my father, who died twenty years ago, my mother, who recently passed away, my relatives, my friends and co-workers. The whole world is there, around the altar. The Mass is never a private affair, even in the most farflung mountain chapel.

With the penitential prayers that begin the Mass, I humbly confess my sins and prepare to receive grace, the only source of salvation.

Through the prayers of the missal, the awareness of God's initiative in saving me is renewed. I receive a perspective that enables me to recognize Christ's presence in the moments of the day: in things, in people, in events – in everything that, otherwise, might be only dullness and heaviness.

The Scripture readings chosen by the Church in its wisdom – especially now that, since Vatican II, we hear a larger selection of texts in our own language – renew in us every day the awareness of being part of a history that stretches from Adam, to Christ, to our own day.

The offertory of the Mass, especially after the insertion by pope Paul VI of the blessings that recall the ancient prayers of the Jewish *Berakah*, is an absolutely essential moment in the celebration of the Mass and in my day. With my brothers I receive the offerings of bread and wine, which symbolize those present, their affections and their work, but also the cries of so many who, though not present, have made requests of me. And finally, it is the cry of all humanity. When the bread and wine are transformed into the body and blood of Christ, all of these requests, these expectations, these words of praise become matter for the edification of the Church. Every day through the offertory, I experience a profound connection between the work and the affections of all those on their way toward the heavenly Jerusalem.

It is the consecration, however, that brings us to the most precious part of the Mass, for ourselves and for those present. *This is my body... this is my blood. Do this in memory of me* (Cf. Lk 22, 19-20). We cannot say these words year after year without their making a deep mark in our being. We know that they are effective independently of our present state of mind, and even of our sins. At the same time, they effect in us who celebrate, as in many of those who will receive the bread and wine that have become the body and blood of Christ, a real identification with Jesus. Through even a single eucharistic celebration, the whole of earthly reality moves toward its fulfillment.

Fulfillment and end

St. Thomas wrote that the Eucharist is the fulfillment of human life and the end of all the sacraments.[30] I think that every priest should meditate at length on these words, digesting them deeply, so as to understand how much he has received from God, as well as how much has been entrusted to him for the sake of his fellow human beings. That the Eucharist is the end of all the sacraments can be understood precisely in light of the fact that it is the fulfillment of life. The purpose of the sacraments, in fact, is none other than to bring about in us the stature of him who is the true man: Jesus of Nazareth, the Son of God made flesh. All of this happens entirely by grace, but not without the cooperation of our freedom. In the act in which we say: *this is my body, this is my blood*, while we continue to be part of the Church, we also stand facing the Church, called to offer our whole life so that what every person's heart desires may be fulfilled.

The Eucharist is the movement of the mystery toward us, God's continual, moment by moment initiative towards

---

[30] Cf. Thomas Aquinas, *Summa Theologiae*, III, q. 73, a. 3, ad 1.

ourselves. His stooping down to us began with the creation, was definitively revealed in the Incarnation, continues into the present and will continue until the end of time.

The Eucharist is the continual presence of God within our daily life. I seem to hear again the words of Archbishop Giovanni Battista Montini: "The Lord has not given us a portrait of Himself, a souvenir, a relic, or a symbol, no: he has given us His real presence [...] love creates nearness, [...] it is communication [...] Christ has made himself present in the fullest way – full of mystery, to be sure – leaving us continually enchanted and surprised."[31] Through the transformation it effects, the Eucharist is the source of that positive movement that carries things and people toward the shores of eternity. It is a light-wave that penetrates, warms and burns all matter, even the most refractory and resistant. Through priestly ordination, and especially in the celebration of the Mass, as well as in their work of evangelization and education, priests become the agents of a great dynamism that sustains the history of the world. This movement begins in the unfathomable communion of the Trinity, and ends by including even the faintest inclination of the human heart and the most hidden realities of creation.

Sacrifice and communion

The Eucharist is the supreme sign of the folly of love, which appeared scandalously, once for all, in the cross. When I think of my more than thirty years of participation and

---

[31] G. B. Montini, *Una legge sublime d'amore. Omelia del Giovedì Santo 1959*, in *Discorsi e scritti milanesi* (1954-1963), II, Edizioni Studium, Rome 1997, 2704.

identification with the celebration of the Mass, two experiences in particular come to mind. The first is the experience of sacrifice, the second that of communion.

First, sacrifice. I cannot say: *this is my body, this is my blood*, I cannot agree to be a mediator of the representation of the event of the cross, I cannot use that pronoun, *my*, without also accepting a special incorporation to the life of Jesus, to a degree which only God decides. Every priest is called to this. This experience is one of the most attractive and at the same time awe-inspiring aspects of priestly life.

Every day we come face to face with the reality of suffering and of evil, two experiences that are closely related to one another, but not identical. Much human suffering arises from evil done either by or to people, but there are aspects and moments of suffering that cannot be directly ascribed to anyone. I am thinking here of innocent suffering, which I often have occasion to reflect upon, whether because of those I meet or precisely because of the eucharistic celebration. Only the cross of Christ allows us, I wouldn't say to explain, but at least to approach this supreme scandal of life. The priest who says: *this is my body, this is my blood*, is asked, with many others, to participate in the suffering of his brothers and sisters, and at times even to carry the cross of one who can't or doesn't know how to carry it himself. This is an important aspect of priestly life, which has been manifest in the most sublime way in the stigmata of St. Francis and Padre Pio, or in the silence of faith lived by Teresa of Avila, Thérèse of Lisieux, Teresa of Calcutta and other saints. Every priest must prepare himself for this, though without being so bold as to ask for a special participation in the passion of Christ. For most of us, it is enough to accept what God gives us.

The Mass is also an experience of communion, the name given by the Christian people to the Eucharist. Just as the bread is made of many grains of wheat, and the wine of many grapes – as the ancient *Didaché* says – in the same way partaking of the bread and wine changed into the body and blood of Christ makes us one.[32] This experience had already been clearly described in St. Paul. *We who partake of the one loaf, are one body* (cf. 1Cor 10, 17). The Eucharist, therefore, teaches us forgiveness, acceptance. But above all it brings about in us the experience of communion, that communion which Jesus came into the world to bring.

Peace is often spoken of nowadays, and rightly so. And it is necessary that men and women work for peace, in families as well as in nations. But the greatest agent of peace and reconciliation is that bread in which is hidden the body of Christ. We often forget this. Otherwise we would have a much higher regard for our ministry, and more joy on our faces. In Greek, communion and peace are the same word: *Eiréne*. The peace that is born of the cross.

Sacrifice and communion: John Paul II in *Ecclesia de Eucharistia*, one of his last works, wrote that "The Eucharist is a true banquet."[33] These two aspects of the Eucharist can never be separated, since "The saving efficacy of the sacrifice is fully realized when the Lord's body and blood are received in communion. The Eucharistic Sacrifice is intrinsically directed to the inward union of the faithful with Christ through communion."[34] I live this every day, finding that the Eucharist, as a sacrifice, demands of me the gift of self. And in this self-gift, communion happens again and again.

---

[32] Cf. *Didaché* (*Teaching of the Twelve Apostles*), IX, 4.

[33] John Paul II, *Ecclesia de Eucharistia*, n. 16.

[34] *Ibidem*.

Confession

When a parish in Germany was entrusted to my community ten years ago, I discovered that confession had not been practiced there for thirty years. Simply put, the people no longer went to confession because the priests no longer spoke of the sacrament or sat in the confessional. A sacrament instituted by Jesus – *whatever you remit…* (cf. Jn 20, 23) – and practiced for two thousand years, had been wiped out. The Protestant reformation had won. I found the same situation in a parish entrusted to us in Canada.

At the root of all this is a massive loss of the sense of sin that begins, first and foremost, in priests. Certainly, a significant factor in this was the reaction to an overly-legalistic vision of the sacrament of penance, along with the tendency to sexophobia that marked its practice by some priests during the modern period. Another victory for puritanism?

Sin and evil become clearly visible only in the light of what God has done for us. They are like a shadow, which cannot exist without light. We no longer have a sense of sin today because we no longer have a sense of what we have received, a sense of God's active presence in our lives. We have lost the awareness of life as a dialogue with the Mystery, and thus even of the fact that this dialogue is missing.

I remember once saying to a person who came to confession claiming that he hadn't sinned: "You certainly don't love, because if you loved, you couldn't say what you just said." God does not love us generically or *en masse*. Rather, he loves each one of us; he willed, created, guides and sustains the life of each of us.

The rebirth of confession can therefore begin only with priests. Where there is a priest who feels the need to confess his sins regularly, the people will find him in the confessional, and where there is a priest in the confessional, the people will return to confession.

For me confession is above all a need of the spirit. With communion and the breviary, it is the highest form of prayer in my life. I too was not taught in the seminary how to truly give confession its proper place in the week. I have had to learn this gradually, through the experiences of maturity and the testimony of my brothers.

Confession is above all an encounter with Jesus: *come to me, all you who labor and are weary* (Mt 11, 28). If this is not our perspective, we will be unable to truly experience the sacrament. The encounter with Jesus has two stages. First he makes us whole, healing our ills, forgiving our sins and restoring our wounded humanity. This happens in the Sacrament of Reconciliation. Then he infuses in us a special participation in his life. All of this happens each time we receive the Eucharist.

A priest who has not discovered for himself the need for penance cannot be a good priest. He will not know how to act, either towards people or towards God. He will gradually be overcome by his evil, becoming tired, disappointed, cynical. The day-to-day enemy of priestly life is not so much big sins, but mediocrity.

Priests don't hear confessions because they don't go to confession themselves. Along these lines, it is remarkable that the document *Reconciliatio et poenitentia*, written by John Paul II in 1984, is almost unknown in the Church. One who does not have the experience of being forgiven will not find within himself the desire to awaken the same thirst in others. In this way one neglects the most compelling experience that Christ brought to earth: *I have come to seek what was lost* (cf. Lk 19, 10). Sometimes it seems to me that in these words I have found another proper name for

Jesus: He-who-seeks-what-is-lost. Isn't this what the word *Savior* means?

The experience of confession requires preparation. In Christianity, everything is like this. When we are going to meet a person we love, we prepare well in advance, and for a long time afterwards our thoughts return to the event. We may no longer remember the words that we said or heard, but deep in our heart we cannot forget the face and the kindness we have encountered.

Certainly, coming to Jesus we should not forget the evil that sin has caused, the devastation that has happened in us and around us, spreading in concentric waves to the farthest corners of the universe. We must not forget how much suffering we have caused Jesus: the suffering of that friend whose desire for us is to be once and for all given over to the truth and happy in the Father's arms, the suffering of him who suffered and died precisely for us. Above all, we cannot forget the suffering of him who experiences our indifference and coldness in the face of his love. *Unloved Love*, as St. Mary Magdalene de' Pazzi wrote.

Confession is closely connected to the relationship that each Christian has with the Church community. Sin separates us from the community, breaking bonds that are mysterious and hidden, but real, since it always damages communion. The inability to receive the Eucharist after having committed mortal sin is a visible sign of this rupture. Confession is the action in which I allow God to receive me, restoring and recreating what has been broken.

Finally, through confession, in which his own sins are forgiven, the priest learns that God always communicates with human beings through other people. Not even the priest can have access to the Spirit without going through the body, which is the humanity of Jesus that continues in the limited humanity of the Church. Only in this way can he teach others that one needs humility to recognize that the mystery of God comes to us through poor priests.

A priestly life without confession is like a day without colors. Little by little everything becomes the same, uniform, and finally fades out altogether. Life's subtleties disappear, since daily habits of evil diminish the spirit's sensitivity. Things no longer disturb or raise us up, and everything becomes one big routine.

But ultimately, all this is overcome by the joy of being received again, as that catechesis on confession, the parable of the Prodigal Son, shows us.

V
Study

Do priests study? In my rather lengthy life as a priest, I have not met many brothers who reserve sufficient time for study. And yet study is a necessity that is born out of silence, almost a continuation of it.

The priest is a prophet. Vatican II affirms this,[35] in line with a very long prior tradition. What does it mean to be a prophet? A prophet is not one who speaks of the future, except perhaps occasionally, but one who speaks for another, who lends his voice to another. The history of Israel is filled with such figures, with true and false prophets. Some were great, while for the vast majority of them we don't even know their names. *In the last days*, one wrote, *all of your sons and daughters will become prophets* (cf. Jl 3, 1). In the midst of the Christian people, which is called as a whole to give witness to God, are priests: they are destined, precisely in virtue of their vocation, to be a sign of contradiction in the world, to bring forth a judgment on life that the world could not arrive at on its own.

Jesus said: *my teaching is not my own* (Jn 7, 16). He is *the* prophet, and we must all share in his prophecy. What an awesome responsibility! Are we conscious of being sent to communicate another's words through our own? To communicate the experience given to us by another? The

---

[35] Cf. *Presbyterorum ordinis*, n. 2.

prophet is thus one who does not have a wisdom of his own, nor does he share in the wisdom of the world, but in the wisdom of God. St. Paul writes: *Because in God's wise plan the world, with all its wisdom, did not know God, it pleased God to save those who believe through the foolishness of what has been preached... We preach Christ, the power of God and the wisdom of God* (1Cor 1, 21.24).

The priest is therefore a man like others, called to speak to others the words of God: words of consolation, of invitation, of judgment. Piercing words, but also words of comfort. To be able to do so, he must have the life that is the source of these words within himself: he must live an identification with the person of Jesus and, through him, with the person of the Father. This is why I began my account of my experience of the priesthood by speaking of silence and prayer.

In this chapter I will address the fundamental ways in which God invites the priest to speak to people: the homily and catechesis. But first, I would like to speak of study. Study, like silence, involves reading texts – from Scripture to the Fathers, from theology to history. But whereas silence has an eminently contemplative purpose – we meditate on the words so as to see, through them, the events they speak of –, study is an analytical reflection. Silence and study are not opposed to each other, nor do they exclude one another. The one, in fact, is born of the other. If I meditate on a chapter of St. Paul, for example, I feel the need to return to it later, to understand it in the context of his whole vision, studying his words more deeply, perhaps even reading them in Greek. And the same goes for many other texts that I might come across in my ministry.

The meaning of study

Why study, when we no longer have exams to pass or degrees to earn, when activities and needs press upon us, when people demand our time? Doesn't study amount to a lack of charity, keeping us from the urgent wounds of those around us? This can't be true. Without extending our silence into study, little by little our consciousness of what we have experienced will dry up. Even among the early Franciscans, contrary to what many believe, when some friars opposed study to humility and poverty, they received the authoritative response that, without study, one cannot feed on the Word of God, and therefore cannot live the religious life![36] Without study words become repetitive and dry, and in the end we become insignificant priests. If we want to know God and ourselves, we must study. Study is a labor that allows us to penetrate our lives, to assimilate that knowledge of Christ and of humanity that constitutes for us the highest and most interesting level of knowledge.

The Latin word *studium* also means work, a commitment born of passion. This is exactly what study is for me: passion for man and for God. I take these together, as St. Augustine did at the beginning of the *Soliloquies* when, to reason's inquiry: "What do you want to know?", he responded: "God and man."[37] He knew well that the one was the face of the Other, and that the roads leading to the one and to the Other intersect and flow together. This is why I love to read poetry or literary texts with the seminarians and

---

[36] Cf. K. Esser, Origini e inizi del movimento e dell'ordine francescano, Jaca Book, Milan 1974, 191.
[37] Cf. Augustine, *Soliloquies*, I, 2, 7.

priests of my community, to deepen our knowledge of painting and of art in general, to listen to music, to study philosophy and theology. Jean Leclercq, the great scholar of St. Bernard, wrote a book in which he summarized all the monastic wisdom that comes from study and prayer, aside from manual labor, entitling it significantly: *L'amour des lettres et le désir de Dieu.*[38]

Study does not arise out of nowhere, but from the experience of a presence. For us priests, study is a deepening of faith. We recall St. Anselm's formula, which in fact summarizes the whole Augustinian tradition: *fides quaerens intellectum.*[39] We should not think that this departure from faith will impoverish or restrict our rational investigation. Faith is not a collection of ideas, but above all an encounter, the encounter with the One who is "the center of the universe and of history."[40] In Jesus the entire universe discloses itself before us.[41] Like no one else, he opens to us the horizons of all of reality, beckoning us to investigation and research.

Study is thus a relationship with things and with people whom we do not yet know, or whom we have known only inadequately: with the present and the past, with the great voices of history, with those who can help us grow. In the striking saying of John of Salisbury, a mediaeval scholar, "We are like dwarves on the shoulders of giants,"[42] and thus we can see farther than those who have preceded us.

---

[38] J. Leclercq, *L'amour des lettres et le désir de Dieu*, Editions du Cerf, Paris 1957. The title reads: «The love of letters and the desire for God».

[39] Anselm, *Proslogion*, Proemium, 7.

[40] John Paul II, *Redemptor hominis*, n. 1.

[41] Cf. Dante, *Divina Commedia*, Paradiso, XXXIII, v. 87.

[42] John of Salisbury, *Metalogicon*, III, IV.

Without denying the legitimate autonomy of every science, we know that all things speaks of Him, the Word of God made flesh. The *Imitation of Christ* reminds us of this, echoing the poet Jacopone da Todi, who wrote: *"Omne cosa conclama*, all things acclaim you."[43]

The Jewish people wanted to see the face of God. In an analogous way, study is the desire to see Christ, hidden in all things. Not only is Christ unveiled through study, but in it we increasingly discovery who we are as men. If all this is true, we can conclude that not only is study a continuation of silence and of prayer, but indeed a privileged form of both.

How to study?

I think we should start from the tasks assigned to us: preparation of the homily, catechesis, the answers we need to give to people. Study involves a long and patient stratification of our knowledge, as well as some choices about what we will prioritize in our study. As I wrote in the chapter on silence, we should look for books that will help us to a familiarity with Sacred Scripture, or that give us a sense of the history of God. Moreover, we should read the works of scholars who, without ignoring the most recent studies, are attentive to the Church's teaching and tradition.

I want to dwell for a moment on the importance of reading the classics. I am thinking here of the works of Homer, Vergil, Cicero, Plato, Aristotle, Augustine, Thomas... and

---

[43] J. da Todi, "Como l'anima se lamenta con Dio de la carità superardente in lei infusa", Lauda XC, in *Le Laude*, Libreria Editrice Fiorentina, Florence 1955, 318.

some of the writers nearer to our own day. These authors were men of their own time, who were able to become the teachers of every time. Precisely due to their ability to grasp what is truly essential to the life of each person, they do not stop at the surface of being, but introduce us into the beating heart of the life and humanity of God. The Fathers of the Church occupy a place of special importance among the classical authors. They guide us into that unified vision of Scripture that has clearly been lost today. As the centuries pass and the Church's history is more and more enriched with personalities and protagonists, the clearer it becomes that the teaching of the Fathers remains indispensable.

Finally, the basic school of study for priests is the liturgy. In it we find Scripture texts, the *sensus fidei* of the people of God, the lives and questions of Christians. I found this expression in Jean Daniélou's diary: "May my entire day be an amplification of the *Sanctus*."[44] It seems to me that these words can also be applied to study. In one of his first addresses, at Cologne during World Youth Day 2005, Benedict XVI said: "in-depth study of Sacred Scripture is needed, and also of the faith and life of the Church... This must all be linked with the questions prompted by our reason and with the broader context of modern life."[45] This is why a priest should not ordinarily go without reading the newspaper. What happens in the world belongs to the history of the body of Christ. One needn't read the whole thing, though, perhaps just the most important articles.

---

[44] Cf. J. Daniélou, *Diari spirituali*, Piemme, Casale Monferrato 1998, 154.
[45] Benedict XVI, *Meeting with seminarians at the Church of St Pantaleon in Cologne* (*August* 19, 2005).

The homily

Regarding the Sunday homily, both a long-term and a short-term prepartion are necessary. The long-term preparation is study, a meditation that over the years is never interrupted. Short-term preparation is done by considering the specific texts of that day's liturgy, asking ourselves what they want to say to us. St. Paul says that *faith comes from hearing* (Rm 10, 17), that is, from meditation. Whereas the Greeks privileged sight, the Judaeo-Christian tradition prioritized hearing. Listening is the basic relationship between master, witness and disciple. To speak to humanity, God became man, choosing the way of personal relationship: he chose to speak heart to heart, to become a reality that can be experienced by people of every age. Since faith is an event, this dynamism is inevitable.

To prepare a homily means first of all to ask myself: what is the experience that I want to communicate? "The Word of God comes to us through men who have heard it and drawn from it; through men for whom God has become a concrete experience and who, so to speak, know him first-hand."[46] In his *Seventh Letter*, Plato maintained that important things must be entrusted to oral dialogue. And Søren Kierkegaard, in *The School of Christianity*, said that Christianity only comes alive through the provocation of a Principle, which reaches the present through the existence of a neighbor.[47]

---

[46] J. Ratzinger, *Guardare Cristo. Esercizi di fede, speranza e carità*, Jaca Book, Milan 1989, 26.
[47] Cf. S. Kierkegaard, *Scuola di cristianesimo*, Edizioni di comunità, Milan 1950, 78-80.

Cicero would not have influenced St. Augustine and St. Bernard as he did if he were not known principally as a teacher of rhetoric. Augustine, moreover, was converted listening to Ambrose's homilies. Direct communication was the tool of St. Dominic, who founded the order of preachers, and of St. Francis, who went in person to speak to the Sultan. The modern period was also marked by preaching: what would Christianity have been from the fifteenth to the seventeenth centuries without Savonarola, Bernardine of Siena, Francis Xavier and Bossuet? And we are all still impressed by the communicative abilities of John Paul II and Fr. Giussani.

We must not forget that *ex abundantia cordis os loquitur* (Mt 12, 34): words reveal what is, or what is not, within us. One can only communicate out of an abundance of experience, which will determine the tone of the words, the gestures that accompany them,[48] the order of exposition.

Before speaking one needs to decide what to say, what to emphasize – to be clear on what the central point is that must pass from me to my listeners. This also means deciding what not to say, or what to save for another occasion. In fact not everything can, or should be said: a homily is not a university lecture. One needs to learn not to say things, so as to give emphasis to what is said.

Speaking practically, I would recommend stating the theme at the outset – for example, by highlighting a phrase from the text you want to comment on. Then, develop it with some examples. It is very important to stress phrases

---

[48] TRANLATOR'S NOTE: Recall that Fr. Camisasca is an Italian who frequently communicates in an Italian context, where specific meanings often attach to specific hand movements. J.T.P.

and words that can be easily remembered. Finally, a conclusion: a summary or a question, a suggestion that would lead to further reflection.

There is only one way to learn how to comunicate: begin to listen, listen to those who strike us. Then, take the risk of expressing what we have encountered and presses within us to be comunicated.

Catechesis and the Tradition

John Paul II, in a famous discourse from early in his pontificate, spoke of the culture that springs from faith and the fruitful relationship that is established between the two: "It is the whole man, in the concreteness of his daily existence, that is saved in Christ, and therefore it is the whole man that must come to fulfillment in Christ. A faith that does not become culture is a faith not fully accepted, not completely thought through, not faithfully lived."[49] Fr. Giussani also had at heart the problem of culture, defining it as the systematic and critical knowledge of reality.[50]

We cannot offer our people only bits of truth, off the cuff answers to particular problems. A person is truly mature when the ideal that moves him becomes an *organic vision* that can address all of life. It was this need, I believe, that led to the development of catechesis in the Church – the way to maturity in faith.

---

[49] Cf. John Paul II, *To participants in the National Congress of the Ecclesial Movement for Cultural Commitment* (January 16, 1982, Rome).
[50] Cf. L. Giussani, *Si può (veramente?!) vivere così?*, BUR, Milan 1996, 83.

In many seminaries and theological faculties, however, this does not seem to be the orientation. Programs are dominated by courses on particular, specialized themes, presenting even authoritative opinions of theologians, but without their being anchored and explicitly integrated into the whole history of the tradition. What is needed is the recovery of a unified vision: "Theology must be able to shed some excess baggage and concentrate on what is essential. It must be able to distinguish between specific knowledge and basic knowledge."[51] Catechesis itself cannot be conceived of as purely a preparation for reception of the sacraments of communion, confirmation and marriage. Rather, it should be presented as the communication of that organic vision that springs from faith.

It is proper that catechesis be entrusted to the laity, but it is likewise important that priests help these collabora-tors reach a unified and systematic vision of faith. Frequently catechists ignore the most important truths of the faith. I believe that priests must rediscover the beauty that is experienced in introducing children, young people and adults into the passionate discovery of the mysteries of faith that illuminate life. To this end, a useful tool now available to the Church is the *Catechism of the Catholic Church* and its *Compendium*.

The priest must, in the official catechetical texts pro-posed by the Church, find the means for the continual nourishment of his own synthesis, and in turn for offering it to those entrusted to him. Only once he has attained a

---

[51] J. Ratzinger, *Prospettive della formazione sacerdotale*, in AA.VV., *Celibato e magistero. Interventi dei Padri nel Concilio Vaticano II e nel Sinodo dei Vescovi del 1971 e 1990*, San Paolo, Cinisello Balsamo, 1994, 27.

unified vision will he be able to continually face new events and be enriched by them, instead of every new thing provoking in him a crisis of foundations.

Through catechesis, the Church transmits the basic experiences that constitute its life. Every generation is called to rediscover the tradition into which it is born, not to reinvent it from scratch, which would require an effort so great as to cause human history to grind to a halt. One can understand the difficulty our society faces today, since the places of the transmission of experiences – the family, schools, the Church – all seem to be in crisis.

Priests can be important mediators in enabling the new generations to participate in the life we have received, introducing them into a genuine communion of life with the rest of the Church.

VI
Fatherhood

The Christian people calls priests "father," a popular expression that I find extremely meaningful. It expresses something that is deeply rooted in our vocation: we are called by God to be mature people, adults who accompany other men and women, whatever their age, to help them grow.

Our society needs fathers. Less and less common is the figure of one who, with authority and a positive, constructive spirit, accompanies his son in facing the battle of life. The fruits of this absence of the father figure are unfortunately seen in the growing insecurity of young people, and in their continual postponement of the end of adolescence. Where there has been no real experience of a relationship with the father, a creative relationship with reality becomes difficult: one endures it, but does not know how to face it. The young person risks assuming extreme positions towards reality, which, depending on individual temperament, could be on the one hand defensiveness, avoidance, diffidence or closedness, or on the other hand aggressiveness or preconceptions.

Insecurity and instability are characteristic of the world of young people today, many of whom see reality as an enemy. They fear going out of themselves. Afraid of what might happen, they insulate themselves, forming little cliques as protection. Virtual relationships via technology are preferred, or, more ominously, they take refuge in self-forgetfulness through drugs or the frantic pursuit of sex.

Carnal and spiritual fatherhood

We must help young people to rediscover their fathers, and help adults to be authoritative, accepting fathers and mothers. This can be assisted by the example of priests and their *spiritual fatherhood*. I use this expression to make it clear that I want to speak here not of carnal generation but of putative: a fatherhood that takes on a person's education and training, even without a biological relationship. This is the great example offered to us by St. Joseph. Just as the Father entrusted the child Jesus to him, so the lives of our children are entrusted to us by Another. Certainly, a carnal father also generates so as to educate. No one generates merely to bring someone into the world, which would be less than human. Priests are also called to fatherhood: precisely we who, in the Latin Church, bind ourselves before our ordination to the gift of virginity.

Mature, authoritative personalities do not mean perfect personalities, without limitations or blemishes. Put simply, such people are engaged in life, enthusiastic about the grace they have received, and secure, not out of intellectual pride or ideological adherence to some truths, but because they have seriously abandoned themselves to the One who has met them, to save them. The lives of most of the young people whom I led to the priesthood were characterized by the presence of priests who did not remove them from their daily, normal life, but accompanied them in it, showing them how studies, affections, difficulties, and plans for the future were all more true, more beautiful and greater in following Christ. It is precisely within an ordinary life that one understands how extraordinary Jesus is. This is what impresses a young person: to see in a priest, not a specialist in prayer or the liturgy, or a good organizer of games and trips, but a true man who has found in Christ the most authentic development of his intellect and his affections.

The basic characteristic of maturity is faithfulness. *God is faithful* (1Cor 1,9), and faithfulness is the highest form of the imitation of God. What most strikes a young person is the faithfulness with which an adult helps him to grow.

Becoming fathers

To become fathers, we must first recognize ourselves to be sons, as belonging to someone. Without this experience, we will not ourselves become generative and creative. One cannot be a father, one who generates, if he has no one for a father himself.

For a priest, that father could be the bishop or other superior, a wise priest, a spiritual father or a friend.

In the first place I want to stress the importance of the priest's relationship with his bishop (an analogous discussion could also be had regarding the superior of a religious institute). There is an institutional side to this relationship. We do not choose our bishop – we find him. Aside from any personal qualities he may have, the bishop, objectively, is the sign of Christ and the source of our priesthood. The bishop could also have a charismatic, subjective side, which does not contradict the institutional side, but enriches it. The bishop can be a father, not only because he is the objective source of the ministry we exercise, but also as a guide to our growth.

For some time I have been convinced that the exercise of the bishop's ministry must be thoroughly rethought in light of all this, with a corresponding revision of his priorities. Bishops should go back to living with the seminarians, or they should at least dedicate an important portion of their time to them. Or, like great bishops of the past, they could choose to live a common life with some of their priests. I am thinking here of St. Augustine and St. Charles Borromeo.

The split between the father figure and the authority figure has, and continues to, hurt the Church. To the extent possible, the two figures need to be recombined. The bishop, who in recent decades has often been chosen for his administrative gifts, must return to being a father. Not only by right, but living and conceiving of himself as a father who offers himself for his children, and especially for his priests and seminarians.

Whoever our father may be, through him we enter the school of God the Father. Indeed, all human fatherhood comes from Him (cf. Eph 3,15). Only by discovering the fatherhood of God can we experience the value of every earthly fatherhood, and become fathers ourselves.

Entering the school of the saints, the great men and women who have marked the Church's life, our existence opens to horizons and depths previously unknown to us. Such relationships in no way exclude the other kinds of fatherhood that can be found in the world, and that reach us through literature, figurative art and music. Tradition is a river of fatherhood, coming to us to make us men.

Only if we become sons can we become fathers. This sums up the greatest experience of my mature years. Through Fr. Giussani I lived the experience of sonship. In a certain sense, through him I rediscovered my own father and, even more importantly, he made me a son to my own sons. I have been able to experience how important, and indeed consoling it is, to be able to learn new things from one's own growing children. Now I learn from those whom I gave birth to. My collaborators of today, who were my seminarians of yesterday, are the people who most enrich my life from day to day.

To become fathers and disciples of one's own sons also means to learn how to forgive. The experience of forgiveness enables us to look at the past positively. Only if we forgive the weaknesses of our fathers, can we teach others to become adults. When we are cut off from what came before us, we cannot bring those entrusted to us to fulness.

The meaning of spiritual fatherhood

Fatherhood is the imitation of God. Jesus revealed the definitive word of history: God is Father, and the texture of Being is fatherhood. God gives himself to man, making him a father. Fatherhood thus means to take care of another, since God is the One who generates and does not abandon, who creates and educates.

Carnal fatherhood is a participation in the work of creation, spiritual fatherhood in the work of education. In a fundamental and profound sense, therefore, spiritual fatherhood means education. It is above all a great respect for the presence of God in the other. It is the art of bringing the other to the full stature of his maturity. Christ left this task primarily to the Church, and thus our fatherhood is related to the Church's motherhood. The Church is the womb that generates children at the baptismal font, feeding and sustaining them through the sacraments, catechesis and mutual belonging. In the Church a true daily life develops, which is the generative source of education. We are only servants of the body of Christ. This all reveals a crucial dimension of spiritual fatherhood: the one who exercises it brings his children, not to himself, but to the Church.

This in fact is the real danger of spiritual fatherhood: to attach the person to oneself, emotionally, pyschologically or by a sort of spiritual blackmail. When this happens, the spiritual father ends up becoming a kind of buffer between the one entrusted to him and the Church's life.

Fathers to human beings

At some time or another, however, everyone wants or needs advice, an opinion, a consoling word, or help in understanding the implications for his life of what the Church proclaims and proposes to all.

At these times, what should the priest do? Above all he must look to the liturgy, to the word that is said to the people, to the Magisterium addressed to the faithful. He is an intermediary, a bridge. He is like an index finger that points to another.

The people entrusted to us must always be able to recognize that, ultimately, it is not we who speak: it is the Church that speaks. Those we guide must always perceive themselves to be called to partecipate in a life with others, a life in community.

The priest is the terminus of Christ's mercy, the living sign of his acceptance, of his patience, of his bending down to us like the Good Samaritan.

Before giving a response, the priest must be someone who listens, who accepts, who gives the person a sense of having found their home. He must be someone who proposes the Church's way, never wearying of misunderstandings, fully loving each person's freedom and his time. No assent to what he proposes that is not motivated by a conscious freedom will bear stable and enduring fruit.

To the degree necessary, he should know how to give specific responses that help people move forward in life. When he sees the need, the priest must also admonish and correct, always having in view the good of the person he is dealing with. He is like a wise friend who helps to discover the correction that God himself wants to give, and to recognize the signs of his miracles in the world.

A priest must never yield to compromises regarding doctrine, but at the same time he must be merciful in the face of errors committed. People need both clarity and forgiveness. No mother who has aborted a child would find any consolation in being told that what she did was right. But neither is it enough to say: "you made a mistake." We must add: "but God forgives you." And we must accompany her in experiencing the meaning and implications of these words.

Looking at Jesus

To become a father means to no longer think of one's time and possessions as one's own. We thus leave behind a comfortable notion of life and, imitating Christ, become capable of giving ourselves and what we have received.

The Gospel is full of encounters. Jesus knew how to move among the people. He knew how to listen to them. He knew how to go to the heart of their need, without ignoring needs that were more superficial. Through the latter, in fact, he would bring the deeper needs to light. Nor did Jesus abandon people, but instead became their companion. All this, however, would not be enough. It could still be merely the mark and result of a good psychological training. More is needed: we must share with others the richness of what has been given to us, and that is not ours. This is why the Lord desired us, bringing us into the light from the emptiness in which we lived. It is why he has given us faith and, finally, why he called us: to be dispensers of his goods or, as he himself says, administrators (cf. 1 Pt 4, 10). To be apostles, in love only with him.

Priestly fatherhood is manifest, as with Jesus, above all in the power to forgive sins. People live under the weight of their sins and remorse, of their past. Only God's forgiveness can free them. For this reason confession and the confessional are a privileged path of fatherhood.

Fatherhood is also shown in the teaching task entrusted to the priest. To teach means to reveal to men and women the merciful plan regarding their lives. We should prepare ourselves to teach through prayer, silence and study. Prepared to speak, we should also know when it is better to remain silent. And above all remember that we are the bearers of a truth that is not ours, and of which we are only servants.

As a teacher, the priest is not someone who knows and has answers for everything. Rather, he is one who daily learns from his Master. Jesus said: *the Spirit will teach you all things* (Jn 14, 26). The priest encounters new problems and new human frontiers in his ongoing dialogue with people, and learns from Jesus how to go with them across these borders.

Our fatherhood finds its summation in the gift of the Eucharist. The celebration of Mass and eucharistic adoration are not mariginal expressions of this fatherhood, but its heart. Through the Eucharist, we become ever more sons, and thus ever more fathers.

VII
Common Life

Affection is central to the life of every human being. This is also true in the life of a priest, which is marked by the choice of not having a natural family of his own.

One of the most serious dangers for a priest is an affective vacuum: loneliness. This can coexist with the most frenetic activity, which is often the other side of the coin. During the day the priest is often besieged by an endless number of people expecting clear, reassuring answers to the widest variety of questions. Today, moreover, with the decrease in the number of priests, God's minister often spends his time running from place to place, from church to church, from meeting to meeting. When he gets home and finds no one, except perhaps the television (the housekeeper of yesterday has almost disappeared), his loneliness makes itself felt. The presence of other priests in the house might not even lessen this, unless the priest is used to this arrangement since seminary and can appreciate the gift of companionship and refreshment they represent. Nowadays in many dioceses, due to the lack of clergy, groups of parishes are entrusted *en bloc* to small communities of diocesan priests, who are called to live together. This is not an easy arrangement, and it probably has no future in places where there has not been an adequate preparation.

And yet, the aspiration to common life is inscribed in the priestly vocation, and indeed in the Christian vocation.

It has given birth to various forms of expression: from monasteries to convents, to communities of canons, to diocesan presbyteries, to religious institutes. If we scan Church history, we see that very often the rebirth of this aspiration in men's hearts, in the most varied and difficult circumstances, was the work of groups of friends, individuals who lived a profound communion together.[52] We must also not forget that the most fundamental expression of this is the family itself, to which God willed to entrust the future of humanity and the basic work of education. God has not arranged it that we are born alone. From the moment we come into the world, we are with others. We need to learn how to live with others, but this is also the only way to learn who we ourselves are. We have been made to be with others, and only become ourselves with others.

Communion

We are thus led to the root of common life, an expression that may sound strange to many. I intend here to speak of common life among priests. One could also say *communitarian* life, but this term seems to me more superficial and partial than the other. *Common life* connotes the reality of communion, the origin and root of every community.

Communion is an expression of enormous breadth and depth: it speaks of how I have been made, how other things were made, of the final destiny of human beings and of all

---

[52] Cf. Fidel Gonzales Fernandez, I *movimenti. Dalla Chiesa degli apostoli a oggi*, BUR, Milan 2000.

creation. But above all it speaks of the very life of God. In the beginning, in fact, when there was nothing, there was a communion of Persons. As St. John wrote, *God is love* (1Jn 4, 8). Everything that He would freely decide to create outside of himself, bringing it forth from nothing, would bear that communion inscribed in its DNA: matter itself, stones, plants, stars, oceans, heavens, animals and, finally, what counts most, man.[53]

The human being bears within himself the promise of a lived communion, that everywhere in the world he is called to realize through participation in the life of those among whom he lives, in the realities of love and family and in the various forms of friendship. The grace of God is present in these realities, giving them the stability of the whole array of Christian vocations.

Already the Greek philosophers saw man as an incomplete being, destined to be fulfilled in another.[54] The book of *Genesis* goes much deeper than this. It shows the source of this tension when it reveals God's thought: *it is not good for the man to be alone* (Gen 2, 18).

Why did God want man? What does our dialogue with him give to the Father that he would not have already had in his eternal dialogue with the Son? We have no answer to this question. Clearly, however, that absolute gratuity of the mutual gift that is the soul of the life of the Trinity also encompasses creation.

After creating Adam, God leads him to consider the world. He wants to show to man the connection that exists

---

[53] Cf. H. De Lubac, *Catholicism. Christ and the Common Destiny of Man*, Ignatius Press, San Francisco 1998, 25.
[54] Cf. Plato, *Symposium*, 189d – 193d.

between all created beings. Adam becomes aware of the bond that exists between himself and the whole world but, at the same time, he feels a distance. He gave names to things, plants and animals, and yet there remains in him a profound sense of loneliness.

God does not want to leave Adam in this state of abandonment. So, he creates the woman. *This one is flesh of my flesh, bone of my bone* (Gen 2, 23), Adam finally recognizes, as if to say: "finally, I now have a 'you' who can respond to my yearning to communicate."

Communion, even prior to being our destiny, appears here as the secret structure of our being. And yet the woman and the man are unable to live out this promise that is inscribed even in their bodies. Claiming to be self-sufficient, they reject their communion because they reject the One from whom they had received it. If God becomes obscured, so also is the possibility of peace among human beings.

Jesus came into the world precisely to reestablish this possibility of union between man and woman, in families, among peoples: H*e indeed is our peace, who has made of the two* |Jews and pagans| *one people, breaking down the wall of separation... that is, enmity... to create in himself, from the two, one new person* (Eph 2, 14.20; cf. Eph 4, 1.6; Eph 5, 21). Jesus' whole life, and especially his death and resurrection, show that the highest form of love for oneself and self-affirmation is to give oneself. *The one who loses his life will find it* (Mt 10, 39). In him, the unity that Adam and Eve lost is reestablished: not only can another "I" enter into communion with me, but it is even necessary for the fulfillment of my personality. In *Genesis* God says: L*et us make man in our image, in our likeness* (Gn 1, 26). These words indicate the person's spirituality – his intelligence, will and freedom. But as some of the Fathers noted, underlying these is the communion of life that is the Trinity itself.

It is not by chance, therefore, that Jesus chose to create around himself a community of persons that he had called to leave everything and share everything, always in respect for each one's freedom and individuality. They were extremely different in temperament, sensibility and social rank, and yet he made of them a unity. After their Lord's ascension into heaven, when the apostles were separated from each other and sent to the farthest corners of the world in obedience to him, what was born of them was the one Church, a single community, even if comprised of many flames. Among their own followers, the apostles did nothing other than live what they had lived with Jesus. They were for others what Jesus had been for them: the sign and instrument of God.

Community

Without the objectivity of a community to belong to, guided by the authority God has put there to lead it, every one of us, priest or lay person, would ultimately be abandoned to our own idea of God. We would end up obeying ourselves, our own thoughts, ideals and projects. To understand and teach this was St. Benedict's great merit: his work remains a point of reference not only for monasticism, but for the whole Church. He showed through his *Rule* and the communities he established that our personal subjectivity – our temperament, gifts, defects, and our entire history – are saved only when we adhere to the objective life of a community, comprised of assigned tasks, a schedule to be respected, walls within which to live, responsibility and hierarchy. All this is the content of Benedict's *Rule*.

Without a community guided by a rule, our life gropes about in the dark. For Christians in general, this means Sunday Mass, daily prayer, confession and communion at least annually, the nourishment of one's faith that comes from participation in the life of a parish community. Priests also have a rule of life, which I have tried to describe in the initial chapters dedicated to silence, prayer, celebration of the sacraments, preaching and the teaching mission.

Now I ask myself: what place do others, the people of the community to which I belong, have in that rule? I am deeply convinced that a person can live his priestly life authentically only if he lives within a *family* in which there is daily sharing. Fortunate indeed are those priests who have the opportunity to experience the beneficial help of a fraternity lived with others who share the same vocation! Regardless of what community we are a part of, the "house" where we live, there should be at least a few times of common prayer during the week. A rule of common prayer is not sufficient, though. It could happen, unfortunately, that even praying together we remain strangers to one another. People who live in the same house must arrange meetings in which they can communicate to the brothers what is happening in their lives. This makes possible the joy of mutual testimony, and can also provide an opportunity for correction. During my travels, participating frequently in meetings of this kind in the houses of my community, I have experienced how such meetings help people open themselves to others, in search of the truth that precedes and surpasses us.

Finally, there should also be shared rest. During vacations together, when the mind is freer from daily preoccupations, we can more easily accept the other and communicate to him who we are. All of this in turn becomes a strong inspiration in facing the intensity and activity of every day life.

Common life opens us to the discovery of the brother as a sacramental sign of Christ. We westerners need to learn from the East what we have neglected through the years: the eucharistic dimension of the Church. Christ accepts me through the one he puts beside me. Where there are three brothers, there is the whole Church. Without this experience our perspective on others, and especially on those nearest us (the *neighbor*, as Jesus said), will ultimately be marked either by an indifference that wants to unload the other as one unloads a burden, or by an effort to possess him and use him to our own ends.

When St. John Berchmans exclaimed: *vita communis maxima paenitentia*, he was not complaining but, on the contrary, indicating that proximity to others is the principal path to our conversion. None of us can know himself, or truly know Christ, except through the change in his life that the presence of others demands of him. Others shape our lives much more than the rains that furrow the earth and polish stones.

The brother who has been given to me as a companion in my vocation is a sacrament, since precisely his difference is the sign of a presence that transcends me and that sets my entire being in motion. Gilbert Cesbron said: "Every great existence is born of the encounter with a great event."[55] In the company of Christ, this event, this occasion, is the one who has been put beside me. Not only through

---

[55] G. Cesbron, È *mezzanotte dottor Schweitzer*, BUR, Milan 2005, 26.

his holiness, but also through his poverty and even through his sins, he continually directs my life toward God.

Common life is not a duty or a strategy. It is the gift that God the Creator and Savior gives to a person, in order that he might walk toward Him. In it the other brothers – those whom I would never have chosen and those with whom I have become friends – are all the sign of Christ's friendship toward us. They are in fact his own person, correcting us, consoling us, helping us, and showing us the way.

I do not want to run the risk of spiritualism or irenism. I am aware of the difficulties and challenges that are part of the life of every community. Nevertheless, I want to state strongly the conviction that comes to me from the experience of nearly 25 years with my brothers: common life among priests, even in situations of the greatest difficulty, represents, with the help of the Holy Spirit, an extraordinary experience of affective fulness, a beginning in time of that promise guaranteed by the Lord to all those who follow him (cf. Lk 12, 11-12).

Every form of common life must have an authority, if we want it to be of help in our pilgrimage among the people and towards God. Every priest should be intimately open to this dependance. Every bishop and superior should train those under them in this fraternal obedience, offering themselves to their communities as tender, decisive fathers who are attentive and able to listen, but also fearless in pointing out the ideal of a life given to Christ, and in correcting what in various ways is an obstacle in the lives of those entrusted to them. To entrust ourselves to a superior does not mean to lose ourselves to him, to his will and vision of things. God is not glorified by our destruction. It means rather to recognize in the other the sign of a will that exceeds our own, to which we must open ourselves and that we must take seriously, because the wisdom of God is greater than what we have understood and seen thus far.

Correction and forgiveness

In common life we learn correction and forgiveness. To correct means to carry the weight of the other, to lead him from the mistaken path to the right one. Correction, in order to be charitable and to bear fruit, must be done at the right moment, if possible when the other is open to accepting it, and not when it arises out of resentment or anger. In some cases correction must be done immediately and in whatever way possible, when the person is in serious danger. And sometimes, we can only correct some people by bearing them in our prayer.

Finally, the ability to forgive arises in us from the experience of being forgiven. *God first loved us*, says St. John (1Jn 4, 19); he loved us when we were still sinners (cf. Rm 5, 8). He continually carries our being from forgetfulness to remembrance, from falsehood to truth and beauty. The amazement and exuberant gratitude that finding ourselves continually forgiven creates in us, makes it possible for us to forgive our brothers. God's acceptance of us hollows out that space in us in which we can accept others. Forgiveness is the highest imitation of God. It is God's work in us. There is no difference or distance that cannot be transformed into unity.

VIII
Friendship

The flower of friendship often blooms under the tree of communion and common life. Friendship has been the most impressive experience of my life, especially of my mature years. I believe that it is one of the greatest gifts God has given me, a gift to be cared for with much trepidation. Its being a refraction of the trinitarian life makes the experience of friendship an extremely delicate event, requiring an ongoing conversion of heart.

Even if everything else in my life were to change, it would always remain true that, qualitatively and quantitatively, friendship has been my most important experience: in the number of friends, in the intensity of the relationships, in faithfulness over time. My friends have been lay people and priests, men and women. Obviously, the common vocation and responsibility toward the Fraternity entrusted to us has made the friendship with some of my brother priests particularly decisive. It is not without reason that I have dedicated this book to two of them.

Friendship over time

Through the years I have tried to understand my experience through the reflections and understanding of some philosophers and literary figures, especially the Fathers of the Church. I could not help but notice that friendship has been the theme of countless books, either wholly dedicated to the theme or in which friendship occupies a significant place. Aristotle, for example, speaking of friendship in the eighth and ninth books of the *Nicomachean Ethics*, maintains that "nothing is more necessary for life, and without it no good is good."[56] The great Cicero, in his dialogue *Laelius de amicitia*, writes: "Besides wisdom, there is nothing better for man than friendship, gift of the immortal gods to his life."[57] He even adds: "If charity and benevolence, which are the characteristics of friendship, are taken from life, all possibility of joy is removed."[58] The word *charity* for Cicero, who was not a Christian, expresses the gratuity that must motivate friendship, whereas *benevolence* indicates the other's good as the sole criteria of the relationship. But what surprises me most is the definition that Cicero gives to friendship: *divinarum et humanarum rerum consensio*, the common enjoyment of divine and human goods.[59] Cicero perceived that friendship is an earthly sharing regarding our journey towards God.

Cicero, like Aristotle, speaks of the friend as another self.[60] One lives in peace and communion with his friend: the goods of the present life and those hoped for in the future become means for nourishing the harmony of the common life.

Jesus chose some with whom to have a closer relationship. From among his disciples he chose the apostles, to confide his mystery completely to them. In the experience

---

[56] Aristotle, *Nicomachean Ethics*, VIII, 1, 1155a.

[57] Cicero, *Laelius de amicitia*, XX.

[58] *Idem*, CII.

[59] *Idem*, XX.

[60] Cf. Aristotle, *Nicomachean Ethics* 9, 4, 1166a; Cicero, *Laelius…*, LXXX

of the apostolic community, we again find joined the two characteristics of friendship that Cicero had already brilliantly intuited: heaven and earth. The apostolic community is the highest school of friendship that history offers. It is thus not surprising that Jesus said to his apostles: I *have called you friends, because I have told you all that the Father has told me* (Jn 15, 15). At the same time, throughout the history of the Church the apostles have represented the most concrete and human example of friendship.

It is not by chance, therefore, that St. Thomas sees in friendship the pinnacle of charity, the disinterested love that wants the other's good, based on a communion of life, goods and virtues.[61] In the *Speculum caritatis*, Aelred of Rievaulx speaks of friendship as the *genus sacratissimum caritatis*, as the holiest degree of love, capable of reconciling the ordered orientation to the good that is the fruit of reason with the kindness that is based in sentiment.[62]

Texts of the Fathers on the theme are innumerable. Gregory of Nazianzen said to Basil: "It seems as though we had a single soul in two bodies,"[63] an expression of Ovid that we find in Augustine, Cassian and Isidore. Aelred and Ambrose, on the other hand, preferred to speak of a single soul in two persons. As a summary of the eastern tradition, I want to cite a chapter of *The Pillar and Foundation of Truth* by Pavel Florenskij. For him, friends constitute a bi-unity, a dyad: "The fact that there are brothers, however beloved, does not eliminate the need for the friend. To live

---

[61] Cf. Thomas Aquinas, *Summa Theologiae*, II-II, q. 75, a. 3; II-II, q. 26, a. 2; II-II, q. 106, a. 1
[62] Aelred of Rievaulx, *Speculum caritatis*, III, 39.
[63] Gregory Nazianzen, *Discorsi*, XLIII, 16.

among the brothers one must have a friend, even at a distance."[64] In such a unity, each of the friends is confirmed in his own personality, finding his own "I" in the "I" of the other.

Friendship and conversion

The discovery that I belong to Christ's history in the world, accompanied by the faces of my friends, makes of my life something great. Through friendship I have learned that I do not belong to myself.

Clearly, friendship is a fragile good: if friends do not accept the need to change, it can quickly deteriorate and even become a serious enmity. On the other hand, when a friendship is true it opens onto a more enduring love, and helps one to love Christ and his Church more. It makes one responsible to the tasks entrusted to him. This is the test of the truth of a friendship: if it makes us freer in dedication, in work and in sacrifice.

There is a fear of friendship in many seminaries and communities, perhaps precisely because of its fragility. For my part, I think friendship reveals one of the deepest aspects of God's method in communicating with us: election, which always implies choice, preference. To address himself to the whole world, God chose a people and, within it, certain individuals. In the same way, we can't love everybody, but only some. To contribute to the world's good we can't do every job, but only be faithful to what we feel we have been made for. Friendship is therefore the

---

[64] P. Florenskij, *La colonna e il fondamento della verità*, Rusconi, Milan 1974, 477.

most striking evidence that God, through the attraction he inspires in our life for some things, some works and some people, indicates to us the path to follow.

I found written in a friend's book: no one has the right to friendship, but it is nonetheless necessary to everyone.[65] Friendship is a gift. It is not a right, nor can it be demanded, but at the same time it is a necessary gift. Isn't this perhaps its characteristic, more than any other, that makes us perceive its divine nature? God is also absolutely gratuitous and absolutely necessary to us. "Life - natural life - has no better gift to give. Who could have deserved it?", wrote C. S. Lewis.[66]

Only when one has entered into the experience of communion can he know true friendship. Communion is an objective bond, given in baptism. It joins us to the body in which the saints live, those who partake of the goods brought by Jesus.

Friendship cannot be lived with everyone to the same intensity. The friend is someone given to us so we that can live communion in a mutual involvement that is both ideal and affective.

True, there are those who confuse friendship with seeing oneself reflected in the other, to the point of seeing only oneself. This is narcissism, which seeks only the approval and exaltation of the self. This is the opposite of friendship: born of fear, it closes one in on oneself. Friendship, on the other hand, is mutual self-gift; in true friendship, giving and receiving become a single reality.

---

[65] Cf. M. Konrad, Dalla felicità all'amicizia, Lateran University Press, Vatican City 2007, 230.
[66] C. S. Lewis, The Four Loves, Harcourt, New York 1960, 105.

Those educators and formators of future priests who lash out against friendship in order to prevent so-called morbid friendships, make a very serious mistake. They confuse friendship with its pathology. Sure, it is easier for an educator to keep a distance from everyone, not involving himself with anyone, but in the end he loses a basic avenue of education and of enjoyment of life.

Experiencing, in friendship, a victory over our selfishness, the hope is born in us that that spark might ignite the whole world. This is why friendship can have no other foundation than the love of God. It is a self-communication of God towards man. It is not a bond among the perfect, but one tending to perfection. It is a school of humility, moderation, discretion and love of the true over all sentiment.

True friendship has nothing to fear from moments of crisis. Harsh words may fly among authentic friends – they are merely the fertilizer of new depths. To live with a friend is a path of humility. Only in this way does friendship become a source of joy and peace. Our friend opens us to new horizons, and confirms us in those that are sure. Finally, we are led to rest in God and in his will, as the secure harbor of our peace.

IX
Virginity

In the preceding pages we have considered the affective experience lived by the priest in his realities of father, son and brother. The priest is never alone. This was also true of Jesus. When he left Joseph and Mary, the apostles took their place. In this way the sons became for him the mediator of the fatherhood of God.

God makes us fathers by entrusting children to us. Through this responsibility, our humanity matures to its fulness.

The experience of love

Jesus, recalling the Hebrew prayer of the *Shemà*, confirmed that the basic paths to our human fulfillment are love of God and love of neighbor. And he specified: *love God with all your strength, and love your neighbor as yourself* (cf. Dt 6, 5; Mt 22, 37-39). Is there continuity or discontinuity between these loves? There have been great saints in the Church's history who have stressed the latter hypothesis: love for God would be so exclusive as to demand the setting aside of every other love. I have in mind certain sayings of the desert Fathers, but also some passages from St. Teresa of Avila, St. John of the Cross and in general of many mystics. I prefer to think of love for God as an inclusive love, to consider that in him we find everything, though obviously through a process of purification and conversion that is needed in order to enter a degree of love that is different than our own. Love for God is consistent with the deepest desire of our nature. At the same time, since our nature has been wounded by sin, every love tends to exclusive possession, if not to morbidity and suffocation. Jesus summed all of this up when he spoke of the grain of wheat that must die in order to bear fruit (cf. Jn 12, 24).

Love for God and neighbor also teaches me the right way to love myself, to learn to see myself as God sees me. To love myself means to discover that I have been willed and thought of from eternity. At the origin of my person is the positive will of God, the same will that willed the universe. To love myself means to enter into this positive vision of life, this benevolent view of myself and of the world. To enter into Mary's *Magnificat*, which frees the soul from every temptation to withdrawal, complaining or depression.

Not only did God will me, but he also wills me at this moment. I can therefore open myself to the future with hope, in complete abandonment to Him. Hope is in fact faith, projected forward in time. Only if there is something beyond the present and, ultimately, beyond this life, can I hope in tomorrow. The certainty that God transcends the present life, because he is Creator, makes me certain that God is in time and is with me. All of this helps to heal the fear of the future that it is the predominant fear of our time.

In this way, little by little, my attitude toward the past also changes. I learn to love those who came before me, the circumstances I have passed through in my life, my teachers, my parents, but also those who have been put in my path and who, in one way or another, have participated in my self-realization.

Love your enemies (Mt 5, 44), Jesus said. In his invitation, I see the possibility of the reintegration of my whole being. Without arriving at this position, neither can we attain a certainty about God's goodness and accept that it is He who has allowed these enemies to act against us. With time, a positive view of our history begins to mature in us. We recognize that God's love has come to us even through the evil that has been done to us.

How can we love ourselves, and hence our neighbor, if we do not start from the consideration of what God has done for us? Our vocation is the way in which God has thought of us from all eternity. I have not only been willed. I have been called to a particular following and intimacy with Jesus. Love for myself and for Him thus coincides with love for my vocation.

This positive perspective certainly doesn't forget about my sins, my sufferings or my limitations. In fact it is the dynamic condition for being able to accept these and, if possible, to correct them. Above all, a positive outlook on myself allows me to accept the fact that God has given me certain gifts and not others, that He wills that I occupy this place in His plan for the world, and not another. If I love myself, it is easier to acknowledge my mistakes. This is an important path in the purification of love, and it produces peace. Romano Guardini writes: "A road that leads to the future, each to his own, departs only from the acceptance of self."[67] In this way I also learn to suffer for my sins. God helps me through the small and large trials that he sends me. To accept them is possible only by desiring in this way to partake of his cross and his resurrection.

---

[67] Cf. R. Guardini, *Accettare se stessi*, Morcelliana, Brescia 1992, 16.

I am well aware that my passions (pride, jealousy, vain-glory, lust…) are opposed to the purification of love: they enclose me in selfishness, instead of opening me to the infinite. Selfish love only sees in others something to be used. True love, on the other hand, makes us look upon others as a good that is not under our control. It makes us desire to know others for who they are, to appreciate them and respect them. It causes us to think of ourselves as inferior to them, making us patient and merciful (cf. Phil 2,3; 1Cor 13).

The transition from selfish to self-giving love takes place above all in the Eucharist and in confession. Through these sacraments, God fills our hearts with his love, purifies our passions and enables us to live in charity.

The other person is always a sign of God. There is thus no opposition between God and our neighbor, between love for oneself, love for others and love for God.

Virginity

A priest's life, if it is nourished by prayer and by responsibility for his ministry, can be an intensely affective, completely fulfilled life. Jesus promised a hundredfold reward to those who follow him (cf. Mk 10,30; Mt 19,29). We must not forget that this promise, which is true for every Christian, was made by Jesus at precisely the moment when the apostles responded to his invitation to leave everything to follow him. To follow Christ is therefore not a negation of life. Virginity is not an absence of affections, even if it involves the renunciation of a natural family and of physical relations with a woman, so as to be totally available to the ministry entrusted by the Lord.

If a priest had to be concerned about his wife, his work, and the support and education of his children, he would always be a man having to find space for his ministry in the midst of other commitments. He could be tempted to accommodate his ministry to the needs of the family, exposing himself more easily to criticism and resentment. He could not easily relocate, nor could he be completely available for the Gospel. Other worries, economic and moral, would infiltrate his pastoral activity, generating conflicts.

I am by no means convinced that eliminating the requirement of celibacy would increase the number of priests. And I am especially convinced that such a decision would diminish the capacity for witness the Catholic priest now has. This capacity results from the possibility he has of using the things of the world only for the kingdom of God, and not for those whom it would be his duty to provide for if he were married.

Family life today is marked by many difficulties. Why add these to the difficulties of the ministry? To this there could be only one possible objection: if we could prove that the lack of a woman's companionship, including conjugal intimacy, would diminish the person's humanity. If this were so, however, we would have to conclude that Jesus was a diminished man.

Can a man live a human life without experiencing sexual intimacy? Or does the Church ask of its sons something that is impossible? Or worse, does it know well that to live virginity is impossible, and require celibacy only so as to better control its priests?

The experience of thousands of priests, sustained by grace and by the example of Jesus himself, leads us to the response that abstention from sexual relations is neither impossible nor inhuman.

The great biologist Jérôme Lejeune wrote regarding the sexual impulse: "As fundamental as it is (the future of the species depends on it) this biological function is the only one the non-satisfaction of which does not lead to any pathology. The same cannot be said of hunger, thirst, and the need for sleep. In celibacy the impulse, which is always specifically directed, persists, but the appetite becomes generalized. What begins as a genital impulse rises and returns to the Tree of Life and to He who created it."[68]

This said, the Church's decision is not the result of sexophobia. Even if in other centuries, especially due to the influence of Platonism in antiquity and Puritanism in the modern era, some sectors of the Church may have encouraged and lived a negative vision of sexuality, the Christian conception of the human being is not characterized by this attitude. Repeatedly, especially in recent decades, the family has found support and encouragement even at the highest levels of the Church. Indeed, not without bitterness does one observe that the Catholic Church is often alone in its continued support of the monogamous family based on marriage between one man and one woman.

What, then, is the basis of the choice, decisively affirmed by the Latin Church from the IV century on, to ask priests not to marry?[69]

The reasons for priestly celibacy are much deeper than those we have discussed thus far. They are ultimately rooted solely in the choice that Jesus himself made, and that

---

[68] J. Lejeune, *Coeli beatus: osservazioni di un biologo*, in AA. VV., *Solo per amore. Riflessioni sul celibato sacerdotale*, Edizioni Paoline, Cinisello Balsamo 1993, 82.
[69] On this theme see R. Cholij, *Il celibato sacerdotale nei Padri e nella storia della Chiesa*, in Ivi, 31.

he asked of his followers. Though he did not marry, he held women in highest esteem, as is shown by his relationships with his mother, with Martha and Mary, with Mary Magdalene, to whom he first appeared after the resurrection, with the adulterous woman and with the other sinful women that he encountered and forgave. He wanted marriage to again shine in its indissolubility, an effective sign of the union between God and humanity, between himself and his Church. Nothing, or at least very little, in Jewish culture led in the direction of celibacy. To not have children was considered a curse. Why then did Jesus make this choice, if not because he believed that it would express, more than any other choice, his undivided heart in loving the Father and humanity?

Christian virginity can be understood only in light of faith. It is the imitation of Christ, the highest form of identification with his humanity. Jesus lived a complete, loving dependence on the Father. The Son and the Father are one; Jesus does what the Father tells him, what pleases the Father (cf. Jn 8, 28-29; 10, 30; 14, 31). This, above all else, is virginity: to live wholly for God, to participate in his will, to dedicate all of one's energies to his kingdom in this world.

At the same time, Jesus gave himself completely to reconcile humanity with the Father: he lived, died and rose for us, giving his Spirit to form a new people. This also is virginity: the indissoluble bond of Jesus with his Church.

The priest also gives his life for his brothers, "he realizes that nuptial union which, according to the greatest masters, is precisely the perfection of the spiritual life ... Marriage was elevated by Christ to the dignity of a sacrament, because the love of the man and the woman already made present in figure the union of Christ and the Church. The perfect chastity of the priest is no longer only the figure of that union, but its fulfillment [...] Nothing, and no one, binds him to or divides him from others. One with Christ, he becomes one with all."[70]

These are the dizzying heights of virginity: identifying ourselves on earth with Jesus' life, it brings us into the mystery of the Trinity, into God's gaze, into His heart. It gives a mysterious, but real incorruptibility to our moments and to our relationships, impressing upon us the certainty that these will not be swept away with time. Virginity is the splendor that people saw in Jesus' look, in his words and in his actions. We should constantly return to the contemplation of Jesus' look upon Zaccheus, upon the Samaritan woman, upon the widow of Nain, on the lilies of the field, the birds of the air: a look that he drew from prayer, from his continual relationship with the Father.

Sacrifice

Virginity is not possible in our life without sacrifice. As I have noted more than once in these last chapters, a progressive detachment must gradually mature in us, from an instinctive way of possessing, to a perspective that loves and respects the other in his or her being as a creature of God. In this detachment from our instinctivity we will experience the dawn of a new life. It is the experience, already in this life, of the hundredfold promised by Jesus.

It is essential to virginity that it be a witness, a *martyrdom* to use the ancient term. A passion that Christ would be known by others and transform their lives too, so that the world would be more human. Virginity is a way of life that cries out the name of

---

[70] D. Barsotti, *Spiritualità del celibato sacerdotale*, in Ivi, 175.

Christ, that shouts Christ as the only basis for and the only possibility of a fullness of life.[71] It is the summit of love, our response to Christ's favor, and in it we learn to love all the rest.

---

[71] Cf. L. Giussani, *Il tempo e il tempio*, BUR, Milan 1995, 21 ff.

X
Mary and Women

Women have an important place in the life of the priest. For many priests, their mother remains an important point of reference. They know that she always prays for them, that she remembers them and is concerned for them. Women often sit side by side with the priest on the parish council, and hold significant responsibilities. Statistically, women are the majority in parishes. And yet, moral teachers of the past inculcated in priests a cautious attitude toward women. Without going as far as St. Louis Gonzaga, who is said not to have raised his eyes even to look at his mother, the saints were often portrayed as vigilant ascetics in the face of the danger presented by women.

I am convinced that a man who has freely chosen to live virginity cannot allow himself liberties in this regard if he wants to be faithful to his promise. But I am also certain that this can, and must, take place while maintaining normal relationships.

Friendships with women are not ruled out for a priest, even if respect for the person before him demands the avoidance of any possible ambiguity. In particular the woman must not be misled, allowing her even to hope for an intimacy and affection that are never a source of joy and freedom when someone has chosen to belong to Christ. We must not use anyone to make up for our loneliness and tiredness.

The feminine side

Without the encounter with the feminine world and an adequate reflection on sexual difference, our vision of the world will necessarily be partial and impoverished.

The human being is by nature gift, a capacity to engage in communion. This characteristic is expressed differently in a man and in a woman: the man gives himself and in doing so receives, whereas the woman first receives, and in receiving gives. Each is a different way of being the same gift. Any unilateral notion would be mistaken, as if the man only gave, and the woman only received. Put simply, a man and a woman give and receive differently.[72] But their gift of self is always a response to something that has been received. This observation will allow us to overcome any logic of power and of domination over the other.

A vision of Christianity and the Church which limited itself to considering only the "masculine" aspect of reality – that of government, leadership, institutional authority, of Peter and the hierarchy – would end up being partial. The Church is not comprised only of bishops: in a deep sense, nor are they even the most important part, because they are not an end in themselves. The hierarchy, like the Scripture and the sacraments, is clearly essential to the Christian life, but like them it is always a means. As St. Augustine said: "for you I am a bishop". What matters is the goal, being Christians: "with you I am a Christian."[73]

What is a Christian? We all have the beautiful necessity of learning the answer from a woman: Mary, the mother of

---

[72] Cf. A. López, *Spirits Gift: The Metaphysical Insight of* C. *Bruaire*, CUA Press, Washington DC 2006, 37 - 58; 114 - 137.

[73] Augustine, *Discourse on the Anniversary of his Episcopal Consecration*, Sermon 340, 1.

Jesus, called by the Council of Ephesus "Mother of God" and solemnly proclaimed "Mother of the Church" by Vatican II. In her we find the essential form of life common to every baptized person.

No one has ever entered into the will of God as she did, from the moment of her "yes" on the day of the Annunciation: *may it be done unto me according to your word* (Lk 1, 38). Preserved from original sin in view of her divine maternity, Mary is more important than Peter. There is therefore no reason why a woman should want to become a priest. Jesus excluded this possiblity, not to take something away from the place of women in the Church he founded, but to recognize their supreme dignity.[74]

The woman in the Church, the woman who puts herself in the school of Mary, has much to teach priests.

Is God a mother?

We must look at woman and at her symbolic significance, to grasp in her what is essential for our own life. God was revealed by Jesus as father: he cannot and must not be called *mother*. Besides being contrary to revelation, this expression could open the door to a pantheistic conception

---

[74] The Church has often made pronouncements concerning the priesthood of women. I do not want to address this issue at length here, but only point out a helpful statement of the Declaration Inter insignores of the Congregation for the Doctrine of the Faith: "The Church is a differentiated body, in which each person has his function; the tasks are different and must not be confused. These do not give rise to the superiority of some over others; they do not provide any pretext for jealousy" (VI).

of God that jeopardizes his transcendence.[74] And yet John Paul I said that God is not only father, but also mother.[75] Clearly, he wanted to refer to those characteristics of God's personality that have been revealed in Scripture and are identified with the deepest movements of the Lord's soul.

As *a mother does not forget her infant* (Is 49,15), neither does God forget us. As *a mother consoles her son* (Is 66,13), so God acts toward his people. A psalm (131,2) speaks of the Lord like a mother with her baby in her arms, like a woman who has compassion on the child of her womb. Each day, in the *Benedictus* (Lk 1,68-79), we encounter God's "bowels of mercy", his womb of pity, translated into English as *tender compassion*.

Through woman's deepest vocation – that of being a mother, of bearing in her womb and protecting, her capacity to welcome, to be a "dwelling", to forgive – we enter into the very reality of God. In this way we understand something of the relationship between the Father and the Son, between God and humanity. The Trinity is a communion, not a family. We are thus very far from the ancient pagan ideas that saw at the origin of the universe the encounter between a masculine reality and a feminine one. But all of this does not rule out that the reality of the mother, a human creature, could bring us to know something about God and about ourselves.[76]

---

[75] Cf. J. Ratzinger - Benedict XVI, *Jesus of Nazareth, op. cit.*, 139-140.

[76] Cf. John Paul I, *Angelus*, September 10, 1978. Cf. also *Catechism of the Catholic Church*, n. 239.

[77] Even St. Paul speaks of himself as a mother. He gave birth to his communities and wants to present them to God as a chaste virgin, without blemish (cf. 2Cor 11, 2).

Mary and the woman

Through Mary we see expressed, and can understand, the particular gift that every woman can offer to humanity, and especially to the Church.[78] In *Mulieris dignitatem* John Paul II says that Mary is woman as she was willed at creation, in the eternal thought of God.[79] At the same time, she is the new principle of feminine life, as it has been saved by Jesus.

The Gospel of John is framed by two episodes in which Jesus calls Mary, not by her own name, but with the expression *woman*. At Cana, at the beginning (cf. Jn 2,4), and under the cross, at the end (cf. Jn 19,26).

In this gospel Mary is never called by her name: the evangelist clearly wants to represent in her the icon of every faithful person, the icon of every believer. He wanted everyone to be able to see themselves in that woman, and to find in her the path to following Jesus.

Nor does Mary's name appear in St. Paul's letters. There is only one reference to her, when Paul writes: *born of a woman* (cf. Gal 4, 4). Once more, Mary is called by this term, *woman*, which could seem generic but in fact is deeply significant. For John and Paul, Mary is the woman *par excellence*, the new Eve, the first person redeemed in the history of salvation, the new creature, the "full of grace."

---

[78] My reflections are born of a reading of two of John Paul II's encyclicals: *Redemptoris Mater* and *Mulieris dignitatem*, and of two small books of J. Ratzinger: *La figlia di Sion*, Jaca Book, Milan 1979; *Maria, Chiesa nascente*, San Paolo, Cinisello Balsamo 1998.

[79] Cf. John Paul II, *Mulieris dignitatem*, n. 11.

If the prophets spoke of the covenant between God and humanity using the image of marriage (cf. Hos 2, 21-22; cf. Jer 2, 2), it is precisely in Mary that the wedding of God and humanity takes place in a real and definitive sense. In Mary, God takes on flesh. To Eve's "no," responds Mary's "yes", which makes her the true daughter of Zion, the people definitively united with God.

Dante, in St. Bernard's eulogy to Mary in the last cantica of *Paradise*, rightly speaks of her as the "daughter of your son."[80] To be a mother, Mary first had to be a daughter. She is a mother because she is a virgin: she became a mother by saying yes. St. Augustine, in one of those plays on words that he was so fond of, wrote that Mary became a mother "prius mente, quam ventre."[81] The "yes" that the whole people of Israel had never been able to say in a definitive and stable way, was now pronounced for all time.[82]

Finally, from Mary we learn the faith that makes us members of the Christian people. We must look to her to understand how to be with Jesus, and how to come before Jesus. St. Luke says of her, relating Elizabeth's words: *blessed is she who believed that the Lord's word to her would be fulfilled* (Lk 1, 45). Mary entered into the promise made to her, which she didn't doubt. Like every woman who, becoming a mother, welcomes a new life in her womb and cares for it to bring it to birth, so Mary welcomed the Word of God that was made flesh in her. This capacity to welcome and care for, which is typical of every woman and Mary's highest virtue,

---

[80] "Virgin Mother, daughter of your Son / more humble and exalted than any other creature / fixed goal of the eternal plan", in Dante, *Divina Commedia*, Paradiso, XXXIII.

[81] Augustine, *Sermon* 215, 4.

[82] Cf. J. Ratzinger, *Maria Chiesa nascente, op. cit.*, 21.

reveals to us how the miracle of faith comes about and matures in every believer.

In the eleventh chapter of his gospel, Luke recounts the words of a woman in the crowd who cried out: *Blessed is the womb that bore you and the breasts at which you nursed.* But Jesus responded: *Blessed rather are those who hear the word of God and keep it!* (Lk 11, 27-28). At first sight, Jesus could seem to be distancing himself from his own mother. In fact, he exalts her. Mary is great, greater than every other woman and every other man because she, like no one else, listened to the word of God and kept it. It is not enough to listen. One must also keep it. While hearing calls for an openness to God who speaks and teaches, keeping the word means allowing what has been put within us to penetrate deeply, allowing it to grow and mature to the point of bearing fruit. To accept the seed that comes from another and make it become a new life. The mystery of maternity contains the mystery of our relationship with God, with Jesus and with the Church.

Mary, model of the Church

To this end Joseph Ratzinger, as did von Balthasar following Adrienne von Speyr, says that Mary is the supreme model of the Church.[83] The figure of Mary makes us see the Church as both mother and wife: a mother as one who generates children, a wife as one who receives the love of her husband, making him fruitful in herself.

The Church isn't a structure that lives by its activities, but a place that continually generates new children. In a Church

---

[83] *Ibidem.*

where there was no longer a place for Mary, Christianity would become a stale bureaucracy. On the other hand, where she occupies the privileged place that belongs to her, beneath the Son, there is always a new generation.

Following Mary, therefore, we can learn the way of discipleship. At the beginning of John's gospel, the first disciples ask Jesus: *Teacher, where do you live?* (Jn 1, 38). They desire to be welcomed, to be received. And he calls, receives, speaks and enters our life, preparing a dwelling for us. It takes time to understand all this, to understand what God is asking of us, the meaning of his words to us, the path he has put us on.

Luke says of Mary that she kept the words she heard in her heart, pondering them (cf. Lk 2, 19). She sought to understand what she did not yet understand through what she understood already. In her the authentic image of the disciple appears: "Mary does not dwell only in the past, nor in heaven in the intimacy of God [...]; she is here and now a person who acts [...]; she goes before us and explains our history to us, not through theories, but by acting."[84]

When, recently, the Missionary Sisters of St. Charles were founded, I wrote these words in my diary: "They should offer a witness of adoration and of hospitality." In them, as in every woman, I see those who can teach me of openness, of receptivity, of attentiveness to life, to things, to beauty.

Mary and priests

In addition to faith, discipleship, listening, obedience and praise, I also learn from Mary basic aspects of the priestly

---

[84] Cf. *Ivi*, 37.

life. From the beginning of her life, her faith was placed under the sign of the cross: *a sword will pierce your own soul* (Lk 2, 35). It is precisely under the cross that she definitively became mother: *Woman, behold your son* (Jn 19, 26). Her being at the center of her Son's passion teaches us that she, like every priest, is at the center of the battle between God and the devil. *Revelation* also presents her this way (Rev 12, 2-4). Mary is the fundamental key for reading the history of heaven and earth: she is always mother and always threatened by the devil, who does not want the Son of God to be born in the hearts of human beings.

Through Mary's yes, the Son definitively decided the drama of history in the direction of blessing. Thanks to a woman's yes, history has a positive outcome, even if it is not yet fully realized. In Mary the woman has thus become, for all time, the sign of humanity's hope.[85]

She continually intercedes for us. This is another key aspect of the life of the mother of God that illumines our priestly life. John Paul II spoke of a mediation of Mary with regard to our salvation.[86] This was a bold statement that sparked numerous controversies, but it is in a text of Vatican II.[87] The pope had absolutely no intention of detracting from the uniqueness of Christ's mediation, but wanted to stress that Mary, like no one else, participated in that mediation. Ratzinger wrote: "No one believes alone, but everyone lives their own faith also thanks to human mediation."[88]

---

[85] Cf. Benedict XVI, *Angelus*, August 15, 2006.

[86] Cf. John Paul II, *Redemptoris Mater*, n. 44.

[87] Cf. *Lumen gentium*, nn. 60; 62.

[88] J. Ratzinger, *Maria Chiesa nascente, op. cit.*, 44.

Faith always comes to us through the testimony of others. Mary lives her mediation especially through supplication and intercession. She continues to do what she did at Cana, constantly obtaining from Jesus that he anticipate his hour, that he save human beings. "To the very end she lived her entire maternal sharing in the life of Jesus Christ, her Son, in a way that matched her vocation to virginity."[89] She continues to be mother, continues to listen, continues to bring to maturity. "There is an introduction of Mary into the most intimate sphere of the psychological and spiritual life of every person, a mutual entrustment that becomes a continual way to the birth of Christ and the form of Christ in the person."[90]

Every woman finds in her "the secret of living their femininity with dignity."[91] Every believer, man or woman, can see in her the road to travel through all of life: "the self-offering totality of love; the strength that is capable of bearing the greatest sorrows; limitless fidelity and tireless devotion to work; the ability to combine penetrating intuition with words of support and encouragement."[92]

For this reason also, Mary is the mother of priests, and our ministry must be nourished by admiration for her person, her beauty, her strength. The Marian litanies that accompany the rosary are the way to come to know her, to entrust ourselves to her and to ask her to share with us her love for the Son.

---

[89] John Paul II, *Redemptoris Mater*, n. 39.

[90] J. Ratzinger, *Maria Chiesa nascente, op. cit.*, 48.

[91] John Paul II, *Redemptoris Mater*, n. 46.

[92] *Ibidem*.

XI
The Mission in the World

For the priest, as for every Christian, the mission coincides with life itself. It would be deeply mistaken to divide our life into a time that is only preparation for the mission, and another time in which the mission is actually carried out. In the same way, it would be erroneous to think of the day as subdivided into spiritual, interior moments such as prayer, silence and study, and public, exterior moments in the world.

For the priest, who must also know how to discern the different needs of each stage of his ministry, every act is public and private, spiritual and material, directed to God and to human beings.

I hope this has been well-illustrated throughout this book. For example: when a priest prays, if the prayer is authentic, he bears within himself the whole world. When he teaches in a school or cares for the poor of the parish, his words always come from God, and it is to God that his action is always directed. *You did it to me* (Mt 25, 40).

The itinerary for priestly life that I have outlined in these chapters might well be entitled: the mission of the priest. And yet I feel the need to say something more, to make some of the points I have brought out more explicit. If it is true that the priest's mission coincides with his life, we must also say that his life coincides with his mission. Jesus, when thinking of himself, in the depths of his self-consciousness conceived of himself as *the one sent by the Father*. I came across this note in one of Fr. Giussani's rare talks on the priesthood: "the truth that has been fundamentally decisive for me, in my conscience and in my relationship with Christ and with the Church, is the reality of Christ as *Sent by the Father*. I have always thought: if one were to ask Christ personally: 'What is your predominent thought about yourself? Who are you in your own eyes?', I imagine that He would have responded: I *am the One Sent by the Father*."[93] What happened with Jesus is also true for the priest: everything is given to him so that he would be for others.

The priest is called to live among people. Other religious vocations lead a person to enclosure in a monastery or convent. The priest's territory is the street, the countryside, the schools, hospitals and prisons.

He is situated between the monk and the lay person, participating to some degree in the life of both. Like the former, he must be rooted in prayer and silence. Like the latter, he takes part in all the changes and difficulties of humanity and of history.

The laity's co-responsibility

The life and mission of a priest are not ends in themselves. They are by nature destined to be fulfilled in the creation of a people around himself: gathering them, teaching them and leading them, through the events of the world, to the harbor of true life.

The priest is, by an intrinsic requirement of his vocation, a pastor. A pastor gives his life for his sheep in imitation of Jesus, the good shepherd (cf. Jn 10, 11).

---

[93] Cf. L. Giussani, *Vita e spirito nel sacerdote cattolico*, in "30 Giorni", (1993), n. 11, 37-44.

Nothing is as opposed to an authentic priestly life as clericalism. One is "clerical" who thinks of his authority as something owed him in virtue of his cassock or his priestly dignity, who doesn't dirty his hands with the things of everyday life or people's problems. He wants to control everything, and thinks he is always right.

The true pastor, on the other hand, loves to see growth in others, and launches them into the world, encouraging them to take responsibility. He does not want to keep them just in his own sacristy.

Vatican II had much to say about the laity, of Christian inspiration in the professions and in political and social life. At times there has been a conflict within the Church that was not part of the Council's intentions. Priests have sought to be like the laity, and the laity like priests. People have thought in terms of power, not considering the common baptismal dignity that makes everyone, with their different tasks and charisms, members of the one body of Christ, of which we are only servants.

We priests must learn to listen to and value the gifts of the lay people entrusted to us, without letting them mimic our tasks. The secret of the priestly life lies precisely in the respect and appreciation of each person's vocation, while at the same time educating in unity.

The most delicate work in the edification of a community is that of calling others to share our responsibility. Some of the priest's tasks can be entrusted only to him. Others can be shared with the laity, and still others must be entrusted to them entirely. The discernment of these three areas is fundamental. The priest cannot delegate tasks and responsibilities that are his alone to others. Celebration of Mass, preaching, administration of the sacrament of reconciliation, listening to people and giving them wise guidance, are tasks that God has entrusted to him.

This last theme, spiritual direction, brings us to a kind of borderland. Lay people can also be excellent spiritual fathers, as we see in some monks who are not priests, and in some lay men and women dedicated to God. Great humility is needed in this area, a sincere awareness of one's gifts and limitations, and a strong connection to the life of the community.

The priest also has an essential role in inspiring and animating works of charity within the community. He is not the only one who would visit the poor and the sick, but he must be very clear about the purpose of all charitable activity in the Church. Our reaching out to those in need, our efforts to respond to people's needs starting from their essential needs such as faith and hope, must never cause us to forget that the origin of every authentic act of charity is Christ. He loved us and gave himself for us. With respect for each person's freedom of conscience, we must bring everyone we meet to Him. He alone is the authentic and complete response to every human expectation.

A priestly life without a public expression of charity would be a sterile, incomplete life. At the same time, a priest who would spend himself entirely for others, forgetting who has called him and sent him, would be a poor priest who would lose himself without effectively helping his own brothers.

Finally, there are areas in which the priest may want those around him to assume specific responsibilities: catechesis, liturgical service, the administration of goods... To generate collaboration means to share one's life, to bring others into what we have most at heart, into the steps we take towards God and towards others. This is friendship, which I mentioned above as one of the deepest experiences of priestly life.

The priest and works

The place of a priest is not only as the leader of a parish. Throughout the Church's history, God has chosen priests to found new communities. It would take too much space to mention them all. I am thinking for example of St. Benedict and St. Dominic, priests who were at the origins of monastic life in the west and the mendicant orders (that is, moving about in the world), at the beginning and end of the Middle Ages. Ignatius of Loyola and John of the Cross are two other priests who marked the Church's life in the modern period. In more recent centuries we find a veritable army of priests at the origin of educational and charitable works, from Camillus de Lellis to John Bosco, to cite only two of the most famous. No priest can plan his own life, or imagine where God will take him. The greatest missionary saints, such as Francis Xavier and Daniel Comboni, lived their travels to unknown lands as the expression of a charity that called them not to stop in the face of danger and the unknown. I want to mention here a great priest who is particularly dear to me, Fr. Luigi Giussani, who made education in faith his life's work. Another great father was Josè Maria Escrivá de Balaguer, the founder of Opus Dei. Priests have also been called by God to political work, among them Fr. Luigi Sturzo, although he was very clear on the distinction between a priest's duties and those of a politician. I have cited him only to point out how strange the imagination of God can be to our eyes.

The 20th century was the century of priests who were holy because of their charity. For example, Luigi Orione, Giovanni Calabria and, in our own day, Carlo Gnocchi and Oreste Benzi. The work of these saints, each such a different response to historical circumstances, was always linked to evangelization. A priest can have no other aim. When a priest founds schools, hospitals or centers of assistance for the poor, when he goes into the streets in search of the least, the abandoned and the rejected, he does so because he feels within himself an irrepressible urgency to have them encounter the One whom he loves. Even when the name of Christ is not spoken, even when the time is not ripe for an explicit evangelization, the works of charity and education are, by their very existence, an effective sign of the humanism that Jesus brought into world. They are the presence of Jesus himself, who bends down to human beings to lead them to the Father.

The method of mission

There is no life more fascinating than that of a priest. Every day he encounters something new. Through his continual immersion in reality, through the sharing of his life with others, he always comes in contact with new and different situations. His life participates in God's own participation in our lives.

To be a missionary means to simply be present before the other, allowing the ideal passion that moves us shine through. Just as Jesus did. In those he encountered, he caused their vocation to arise. Every word of his, every gesture, had this purpose: to gradually lead them to discover their name, the look with which God loved them.

When St. Paul writes: *God wants all to be saved and come to a knowledge of the truth* (1Tm 2, 4), he is referring to all that Jesus said and manifested in his life, to his way of entering into relationships with people, and to the infinite depth of his sacrifice and his resurrection.

To share is not simply to accept. If we had nothing new to bring to others, we would descend to their level and end by sharing nothing. What we have received is priceless. The more this experience is alive in us, the more others will perceive its newness, and how it would benefit themselves as well.

How is it possible to live on the level of others, to immerse ourselves in their life, and at the same time be something significant for them? What allows us to *be all things to all people* (cf. 1Cor 9, 22), without disappearing, without losing ourselves in them, but instead being that salt for others' lives that Jesus spoke of (cf. Mt 5, 13)? The Spirit of Christ can do all this. Through his work, opposites are united, what is far away becomes near, the enemy becomes a brother, our eyes are opened to the incomprehensible. And in this way, all things are ours.

Every priest is sent to all people. He relives the life of Jesus, who was made like us in all things, binding himself to the humility of our condition.[94] In this way we are invited to break down the barriers that divide us from others, to overcome the strategies by which we try to placate ourselves in the face of the provocation that Christ offers to our life through others' inexhaustible diversity.

The other is a part of Christ, and thus of ourselves, that we do not yet know. Mission, therefore, is not something that is added to our experience of Christ, but the continual broadening and deepening of that first moment in which He invited us to follow him.

---

[94] Cf. Benedict XVI, *Angelus*, January 1st 2006.

XII
Who is the Priest?

Who is the priest? An ordinary man, a sinner like others, invested with a power so extraordinary as to be able to change bread and wine into the body and blood of Christ; called by a vocation so sublime as to make of him a bridge between heaven and earth: *whatever you loose on earth will be loosed in heaven* (cf. Mt 16, 19). It is not surprising, therefore, that the figure of the priest has been, and continues to be, portrayed in literature and film.

One thinks of Chesterton's *Father Brown*, of Marshall and *Father Smith*, of Bernanos's spiritual *country priest* or, at the opposite end of the spectrum, Graham Greene's materialistic priest in *The Power and the Glory*, or don Abbondio, or Father Christopher in Manzoni's *The Betrothed*, or Guareschi's *don Camillo*, Father Barry of *On the Waterfront*, or the priest in Hitchcock's *I Confess*.

Why such curiosity – and such anger – if not that the priest is a strange being, at the border of the worlds of good and evil?

Chosen by God from among men

Attractive though it may be, I do not want to pursue the path suggested by these artistic investigations. Rather, I wish to look directly at what has happened to me – at what I have seen and continue to see being lived in hundreds and hundreds of priests, many of them the young people that I myself have accompanied toward the priesthood.

If I look at my own experience, there is no doubt: the priest is a man chosen by God from among other men to be an instrument of his mercy towards them. In this way the Father makes the priest participate in the very life of Jesus. During a pilgrimage that lasts his entire life, little by little the priest accepts in himself the very proportions of the heart of Christ, his thoughts, his missionary thirst.

For this reason he accepts the fact that he no longer has time of his own to shape according to his pleasure, or goods to use as he will, or affections that can entirely control his life. And yet the priest is not a man outside the world, an insensitive being – much less a man without sentiments. On the contrary, he is dominated by a passion that makes him a part of everything, curious about everything, attentive to all that happens in the world about him, both near and far. He has everything he needs to be a true, complete man.

A *sign of mercy*

I have often thought of the last years of John Paul II's life. He was a great priest, a lover of Christ, an evangelizer with a profound knowledge of man in his misery and his greatness. Throughout his intense life, he wanted to sum up, with a single word, what God is: mercy.[95] And Karol Wojtyła received the grace of dying on the vigil of the feast of Divine Mercy, instituted by him.

---

[95] Cf. John Paul II, *Dives in misericordia*.

Why, and how, is the priest a sign of mercy? Above all because he has received from Jesus the power to forgive sins, and to make present the body and blood of Christ. This is the royal way along which God travels to save human beings, the way opened by the cross.

Jesus came to seek those who were lost. Like him, the priest must not wait for people in church, as though he had the right to expect that others would come to him. Rather, he must enter all the environments in which his contemporaries live. Paradoxically, in the past the Church was more present in the various contexts of life than today – in hospitals, in schools, among the young. Today there is a private notion of faith, as if to say: "The world belongs to humanity, the sacristies to God." Certainly, this work of presence belongs especially to the lay faithful. The fact remains, however, that the priest is sent by Jesus to all people of the world, in whatever situation they live in. *Even the saints go to hell*, wrote Cesbron, referring to the French worker-priests of the 1900's. Clearly, the priority belongs to those who are most needy: the little ones, the poor, sinners. The lonely, the abandoned, those sick in body or in spirit, without hope, slaves of their passions – these are the priest's continual companions. But Jesus came for all: he ate with prostitutes and with rich publicans, not fearing the judgment of convention. In the same way, the priest must go to the poor and to the rich, to the ignorant and the learned, to the disinherited and the powerful.

Where will he find the courage, the spiritual strength to continually reach out to human beings? Where will he find the energy to continually stoop to new wounds, without falling into a limitless weariness or, even worse, into a disillusionment of soul that could lead him to discouragement and ultimately to scandal?

Only in the certainty of being one who has received mercy, and who continually receives it.

Humility and holiness

Meekness, humility, poverty of spirit are the words Jesus used to express the paradox of his followers' courage. St. Paul also speaks of strength and weakness: *It is when I am weak that I find strength within me* (cf. 2Cor 12, 10).

Humility is a fundamental path of the priestly life. The word derives from *humus*, "earth" in Latin. Humility is thus an objective consideration of one's gifts and limitations, knowing how to attribute the former to God as their true source, and to calmly recognize the latter, without yielding to pride. It is a long road, on which one must always begin anew — a road that identifies us with Jesus' soul. He *did not consider his equality with God something to be grasped*, but, *humbled himself to the point of taking on our flesh* (cf. Phil 2, 6-8). An abyss of humility that we can only glimpse from afar.

So, humility has nothing to do with false affectation, with a failure to recognize our gifts: on the contrary, it is a virile and realistic virtue that makes one secure.

Holiness, like humility, also produces great balance. True, holiness always has something in it of folly, of exaggeration beyond our inadequate categories. The life of a saint is not a life of comfort, lived in an aura of goodness and serenity. It is also true, however, that Christian holiness, even in exceptional cases like St. Francis, Padre Pio, Mother Teresa of Calcutta, always has the coloring of everyday life. From the moment when God became man, our relationship with him has been decided entirely in the details, which can often be overlooked by human eyes. *Our life is decided entirely in the greatness with which we live what is small.* Holiness has to do with what God is asking of me at this moment. For the priest: to attend to his ministry. *Age quod agis*, the Romans said. "Imitate what you handle", as the *Pontificale Romanum* says,[96] speaking of the Eucharist. In his ministry, the priest has all the paths necessary for his holiness – which is to say, for his self-realization.

He must remember, however, that it is not enough simply to fulfill the actions commanded or required of him. He must enter into the Spirit of the One who has commanded them.

Clearly, the apostolic priestly life is an active one. But our efforts will not save us if contemplation, silence, prayer, the growing and continual discovery of the will of God are not the soul that informs our action.

To be able to launch out into the world, the priest has a need at once demanding and profound, sweet and mysterious, like a hunger, or a thirst: to root himself in God. This rootedness is born of the certainty that he is not a priest by his own will. No one can become a priest simply because he wants to. Rather, he becomes one because he is called, and because his vocation has been evaluated over time by the Church, and in the end affirmed.

Obedience and poverty

All of this points to a fundamental desire in the life of the priest: obedience.

Obedience has nothing in common with the unloading of the responsibility for one's actions onto someone else; nor is it a reduction of one's freedom, or the loss of one's

---

[96] Cf. *Pontificale Romanum. De ordinatione episcopi, presbyterorum et diaconorum*, n. 123.

will to another. Obedience is born, rather, of the awareness that to live is to participate in a design that precedes us, to adhere to a life that has been given to us, to enter a history of which we must first of all be servants – if in the end we wish to reign. As the mediaevals put it: *servire Deo, regnare est. The most serious problem of the post-conciliar period has been the loss of the sense of obedience.* Its rationale is no longer understood – indeed, it is often seen as an enemy. *Obedience is not a virtue,* wrote Fr. Milani. He was right to point out that obedience is more or less impossible if it doesn't take place in the context of a communion of ideals, of projects, of sacrifices: the communion that is God, who sends his Son into the world, who in turn sends the apostles. But without obedience, there is no Church. At most, there is an assortment of good intentions.

Many priests today experience obedience as a negative virtue, as a diminishing of their personality. A new perspective is needed: through obedience, I participate in the Church's whole history, I enter into relation with those who went before me, I partake of their wisdom. But especially I recognize myself as part of a people that is greater than me, guided by God through those He has chosen. In the first place, this means Peter and his successors, and with him the bishops.

The world's history does not begin with me. Even if each man is called to make his own creative contribution to the human community – to re-elaborate, not in mere passive acceptance, what has been passed down to him – it is also true that no one can consider himself the owner of the tradition he has received. I must therefore vitally enter into it, and in turn pass it on to those who come after me.

Cardinal Lercaro and other prelates had the great merit, during the Second Vatican Council, of calling the Church's attention to the reality of the poor and of *poverty* in the Church. Since then, poverty has been a theme much debated, but little lived. The sociological and political dimension has prevailed, at the expense of the properly Christian dimension.

In the message of many missionaries, and even that of many bishops, the "poor" have supplanted the fact and ideal of Christian poverty. Some think it necessary to resolve the problem of the economic and cultural condition of destitute millions before it is possible to tell them that Christ is the only hope in life. This has led to a pro-Marxist tendency in theology and pastoral activity, with devastating effects on the Christian conscience of entire peoples, especially in Latin America, but also in Africa. On the other hand, in the rich countries of the West, the organized charity of many churches, efficient and "agency-based", has obscured the need to educate Christians in the beauty of evangelical poverty. Even in the Church, poverty is a word that for most people today means only material indigence.

Poverty consists, rather, in the great discovery that in Christ we have all received, and continue to receive, everything necessary for life: faith, a new knowledge of the world, charity that makes us capable of loving, and hope that makes possible the battle of daily life, and a constructive boldness. Everything else is either a function of these goods or is unnecessary. And what is unnecessary can be done without, in order to live with Christ and as Christ.

How beautiful it is to enter the house of a priest and find it sober, clean, orderly! Unfortunately this is not always the case. Even how one dresses has its importance, and how one eats. Neglect, disorder, and slovenliness have nothing to do with authentic poverty, which is always lived with a certain joy, or at least a certain gladness of heart, conferring dignity and beauty even on the renunciation of material goods.

Servus servorum

During the Sixties and Seventies, I often heard "service" spoken of within the Church. I even developed a certain dislike for the word: its sociological connotations bothered me. In later years, however, I gradually rediscovered it. Today, taught by St. Augustine, I find that it expresses very well the priestly identity, both in relation to Christ and to the Church. Indeed, the word *servant* allows us to enter into the very reality of the Trinity, into Christ's relationship with the Father.

"If the priest is defined as the servant of Jesus Christ, then his existence is essentially relational [...] He is a servant of Christ, so as to be, from him, with him and for him, a servant of human beings."[97]

As Christ lived his entire existence in relation with the Father, so the priest does not belong to himself. His life is not his own. Rather, his life mediates an initiative that comes from another. He has been taken captive by Christ, for a task that Christ wants to entrust to him.[98]

The fact that priests belong to Christ means that they are his servants, called to give something they could never give on their own. What priests offer does not come from themselves: not the words they say, nor their actions, nor what their words and actions mean and accomplish. It is Christ who speaks and acts through the priest.

---

[97] J. Ratzinger, *Il ministero e la vita dei presbiteri*, in "Studi Cattolici", 40 (1996), 327.
[98] Cf. *Ivi*, 328.

Christ's expression *useless servants* (Lk 17, 10) is very eloquent. One is a useless servant not because what he does is unimportant, but because the ultimate meaning of his service is not in what he does. It is in his availability to others. The priest is a useless servant in that he is called to make a gift of his whole being to Him from whom he first received it.

In this way he becomes the servant of the Christian people. Jesus does not want the people gathered around him to be deprived of his gifts, without a constant relationship with himself. He therefore entrusts priests with the task of participating in the ministry through which he creates, guides and educates his people.

As Christ gave and gives his life for his own, in the same way he asks every priest to give himself for the Church – and in this way the priest finds his own happiness.